BRILLIANT
BRITISH
HISTORY

BRILLIANT BRITISH HISTORY

Fiona Macdonald,

Jeremy Smith, Philip Steele

Miles Kelly

First published in 2011 by Miles Kelly Publishing Ltd
Harding's Barn, Bardfield End Green, Thaxted, Essex, CM6 3PX, UK

2 4 6 8 10 9 7 5 3 1

Publishing Director Belinda Gallagher
Creative Director Jo Cowan
Editorial Assistant Lauren White
Cover Designer Simon Lee
Designers Joe Jones, Andrea Slane
Additional Design Kayleigh Allen
Image Manager Liberty Newton
Production Manager Elizabeth Collins
Reprographics Stephan Davis, Jennifer Hunt, Anthony Cambray

ISBN 978-1-84810-462-4

Printed in China

British Library Cataloguing-in-Publication Data
A catalogue record for this book is available from the British Library

Made with paper from a sustainable forest

www.mileskelly.net   info@mileskelly.net

www.factsforprojects.com

Self-publish your
children's book

buddingpress.co.uk

CONTENTS

BRITISH HISTORY

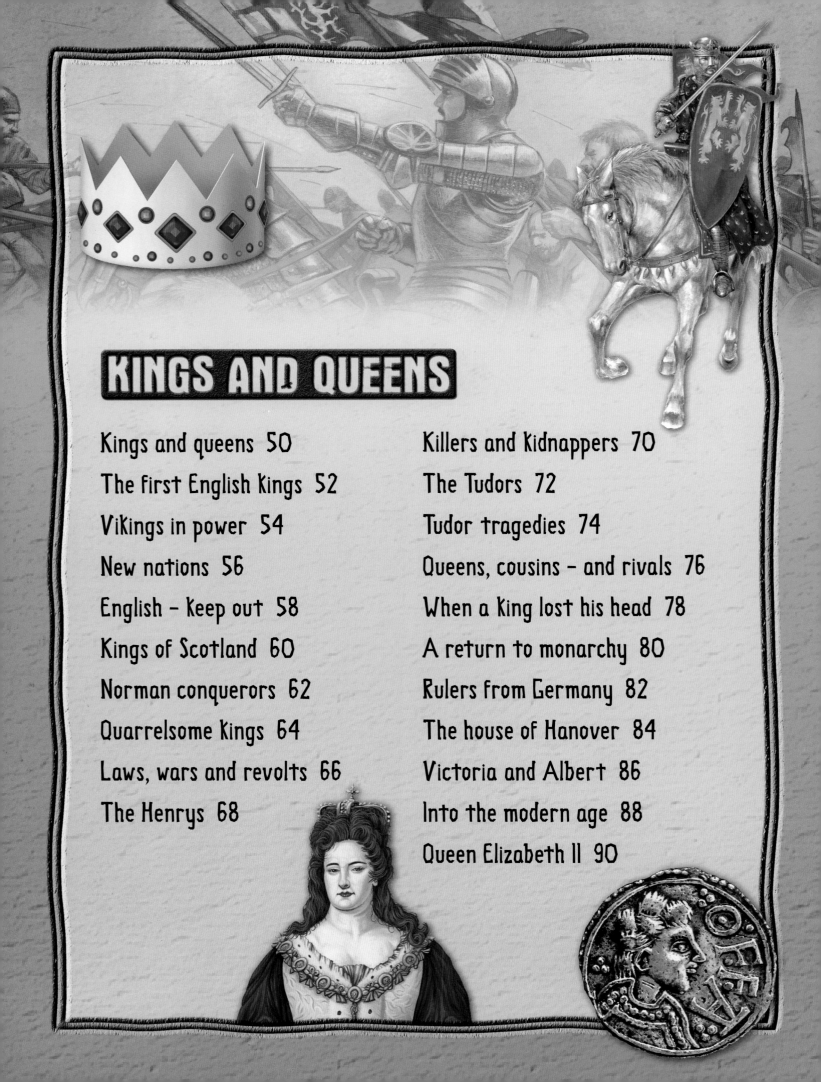

KINGS AND QUEENS

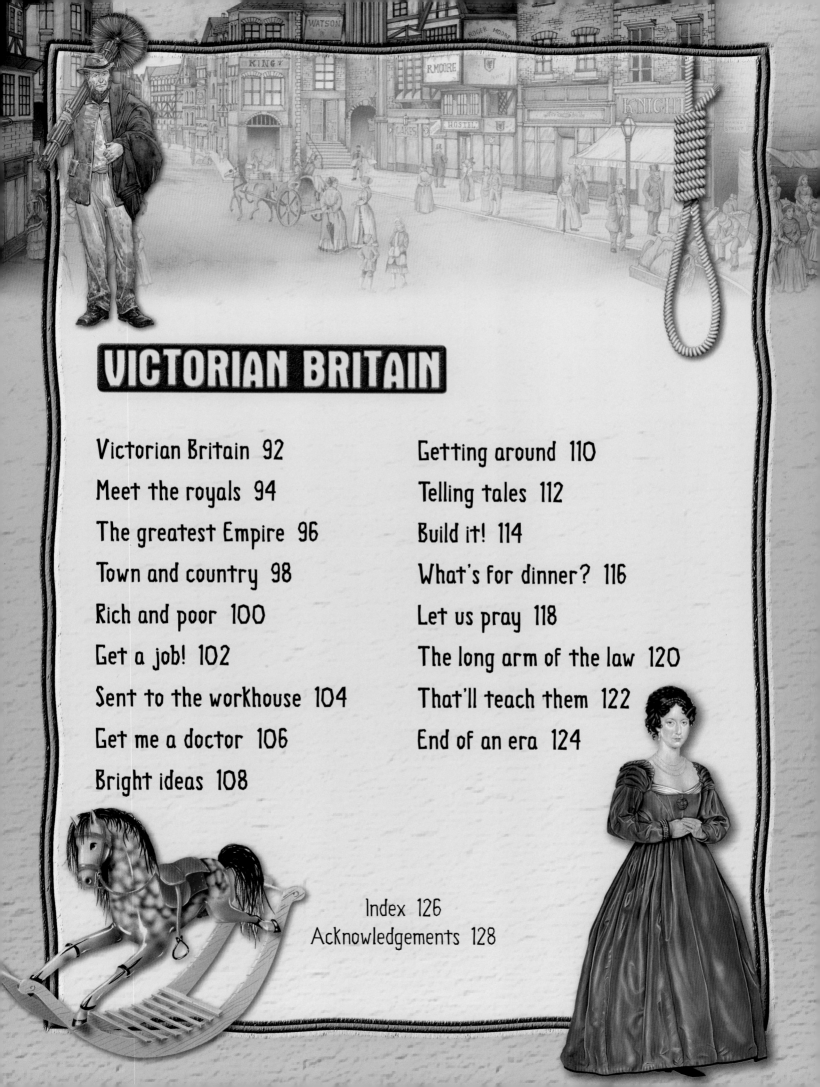

VICTORIAN BRITAIN

Human beings like us were living in Great Britain about 37,000 years ago. They hunted animals, caught fish and gathered plants they could eat. They used simple tools and weapons made of stone and wood. Britain was not an island then, but part of mainland Europe. The weather was often very cold and the land became covered in ice for long periods of time. The last of these ice ages ended about 10,000 years ago. As the weather became warmer, the ice melted and the sea level rose. Britain became an island.

▶ As the last ice age ended and the climate became warmer, bands of hunters moved into new woodlands and wetlands. As well as deer, fish and shellfish were important food sources.

Stone and bronze

▼ Animals didn't just provide meat for food. Their skins were scraped clean with flint tools and then sewn together using bone needles to make clothing and tents.

By 6000 BC, hunters in Britain had become skilled at making tools and weapons such as needles, fish hooks and harpoons. They hunted deer, boar and wild oxen in the oak forests. They used animal skins to make clothes and coverings for shelters.

▶ Careful chipping could turn a flint into a razor-sharp tool or weapon.

Flint was an excellent stone for making tools. It could be chipped and flaked until it was razor-sharp, like glass. The flints lay buried in chalk, so miners had to dig deep, as far as 10 metres down, to reach the best ones. The miners dug the flints out using deer antlers as picks.

▲ The skeletons of flint miners have been found buried in flint mines.

Farming had reached the British Isles by about 4000 BC. Villagers learned to raise sheep and goats. They grew wheat, which they harvested with stone tools. Then they ground the grain into flour. The bread may have been gritty and the animals may have been thin and bony, but it was easier than hunting!

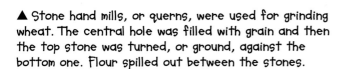

▲ Stone hand mills, or querns, were used for grinding wheat. The central hole was filled with grain and then the top stone was turned, or ground, against the bottom one. Flour spilled out between the stones.

Metal tools and weapons were better than stone ones. Copper

was used in Britain by 2500 BC. About 600 to 700 years later, people discovered how mixing copper with tin made a tough metal mixture, or alloy, called bronze.

▶ Molten (hot, liquid) bronze could be poured into stone moulds. The mould was smeared with soot and grease to give a smooth finish. When the bronze had cooled and hardened, the mould was knocked away.

I DON'T BELIEVE IT!

Some of the pillars at Stonehenge weighed as much as 20 elephants! People hauled them all the way from southwest Wales, a distance of over 215 kilometres.

Between 3000 BC and 1500 BC, massive pillars of stone were used to create a circle at Stonehenge in southern England. The stones were

placed so that they lined up with the rising and setting Sun. It is thought that people used Stonehenge to study the Sun, Moon and stars, as well as to observe the seasons. People would have crowded into the circle on a midsummer morning to watch the rising of the Sun.

The ancient Celts

Around 600 BC, small bands of warriors and traders from mainland Europe began to settle in parts of the British Isles. Many of them belonged to a people called the Celts. Those people already living in the British Isles slowly took on the Celtic way of life. They began to speak Celtic languages, too.

▲ The Celts gradually brought their way of life to many parts of Europe. The three main groups in the northwest of Europe were the Gauls of France, the Gaels of Ireland and the Britons of Great Britain.

MAKE CELTIC COINS

You will need:
coins   heavy card   silver/gold paint   black felt-tip pen   scissors

1. Draw circles around modern coins onto heavy card.
2. Cut out the circles and paint them silver or gold.
3. When the paint is dry, draw your own designs with a black felt-tip pen. Celtic coins were decorated with horses, the heads of gods, or moons and stars.

The ancient Celts were famous for being show-offs. Celtic warriors sometimes wore their hair in spikes, tattooed their skin and wore heavy gold jewellery. Unlike most men in Europe at that time, they wore trousers beneath a short tunic. Women wore long dresses of wool or linen and used mirrors of polished bronze.

► The Celts made beautiful gold bracelets, such as this, and rings and brooches.

The safest place to be when war broke out was on top of a hill or on a headland by the coast. These places could easily be defended from attack with ditches and high wooden fences. Ancient Celts often used hill forts like these. The Celts were great fighters and cattle raiders. They used chariots and fought with long swords.

▶ This great hill fort was at Maiden Castle in Dorset, England. It was protected by timber fences and banks of earth.

Settlement

Timber fence

Bank of earth

The Celts were first-rate metal workers. They knew all about iron. In fact iron was such a hard, useful metal that people who had not seen it before thought it must be magic. Some people still nail iron horseshoes onto doors for good luck.

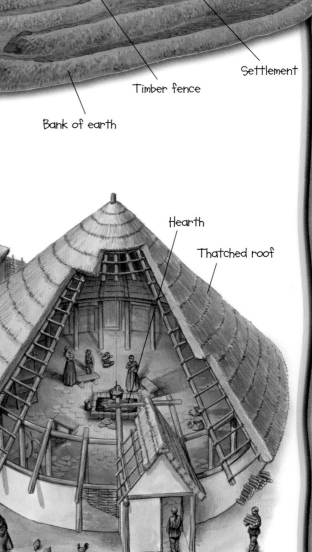

Hearth

Thatched roof

▶ A smoky hearth was the centre of every Celtic round house.

Timber poles

Many British Celts lived in villages, in large round houses. The walls were made of timber and clay, or stone. Inside each house was a fire. The smoke rose through a hole in the thatched roof. The Celts were farmers and blacksmiths and enjoyed hunting too. Their priests and lawmakers were called druids.

Roman Britain

An army of 10,000 Roman soldiers landed in England in 55 BC, led by general Julius Caesar. Despite defeating the Gauls in France, the landing was not a success and the Romans returned to Gaul. In 54 BC the Romans came back with 27,000 soldiers. They marched north to the River Thames and forced the people there to pay money to Rome.

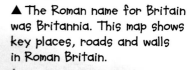

◀ Roman coins are still found in Britain today.

The Romans returned yet again in AD 43 and this time they stayed. They conquered all of Britain except for the north of Scotland, where they built the Antonine Wall to keep the Highlanders out. In AD 122, the Roman's built Hadrian's Wall. This was the northern border of an empire that stretched from Spain, to North Africa and the Black Sea.

▲ The Roman name for Britain was Britannia. This map shows key places, roads and walls in Roman Britain.

In AD 60 there was a bloody revolt against Roman rule, led by a queen called Boudicca. She burned down Roman towns. When her warriors were defeated, she killed herself in despair. Rich Britons now learned to live like Romans. Poorer Britons carried on farming and trading, much as they always had done.

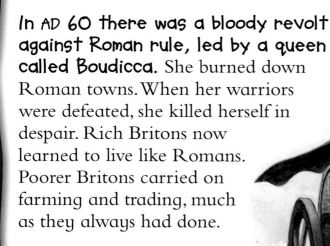

▶ Boudicca led her armies to war against Rome and burned down London.

The Romans liked their comforts. They built public baths where people could have a cold or hot dip, a work-out or a massage. Rich people lived in luxurious country-houses called villas. These even had under-the-floor central heating.

◄ Floors were often decorated with tile pictures called mosaics.

I DON'T BELIEVE IT!

The Romans' secret weapon of war was ... a tortoise! 'Tortoise' was the name given to a group of soldiers who crouched under linking shields to attack a hill fort. Enemy spears just bounced off the top and sides of the tortoise's 'shell'.

Roman soldiers began to leave Britain in AD 401. Many parts of the great empire were now under attack. In Britain there were rebellions. Pirates sailed the seas. The Irish attacked western shores. The city of Rome itself was captured by German warriors in AD 476.

The Romans built long, straight roads from one town to the next. They were built using layers of sand and gravel, paved with stone. In fact, there were no better roads in Britain until the 1800s.

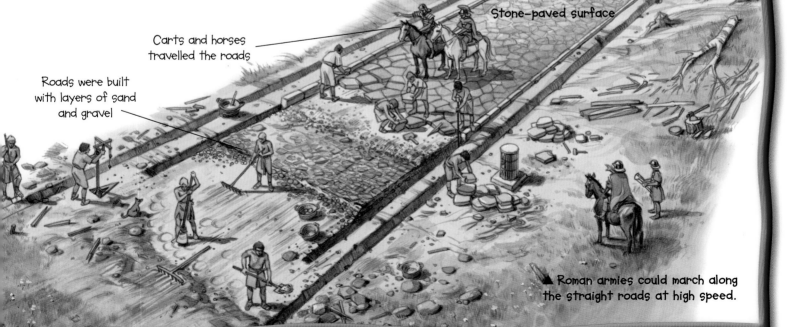

Carts and horses travelled the roads

Stone-paved surface

Roads were built with layers of sand and gravel

▲ Roman armies could march along the straight roads at high speed.

The Anglo-Saxons

▲ This Anglo-Saxon helmet dates from about AD 625.

During the last days of the Roman Empire, raiders from northern Germany began to attack eastern Britain. More and more of them landed in the 400s and 500s. They belonged to various peoples known as Angles, Saxons, Jutes and Frisians. We call them all Anglo-Saxons. Their speech became the English language, mixed with Celtic and Latin.

▲ It took many years for the Anglo-Saxons to conquer much of the area now known as England. They divided it into many separate kingdoms.

▶ The Anglo-Saxons slowly conquered the southern and eastern lands of the British Celts. Armed warriors may have carried a long knife called a sax.

Sax

The invaders carried swords, axes and long knives. They burned down Celtic villages and old Roman towns and set up many small kingdoms. They built small villages of rectangular thatched houses and lived by farming and fishing.

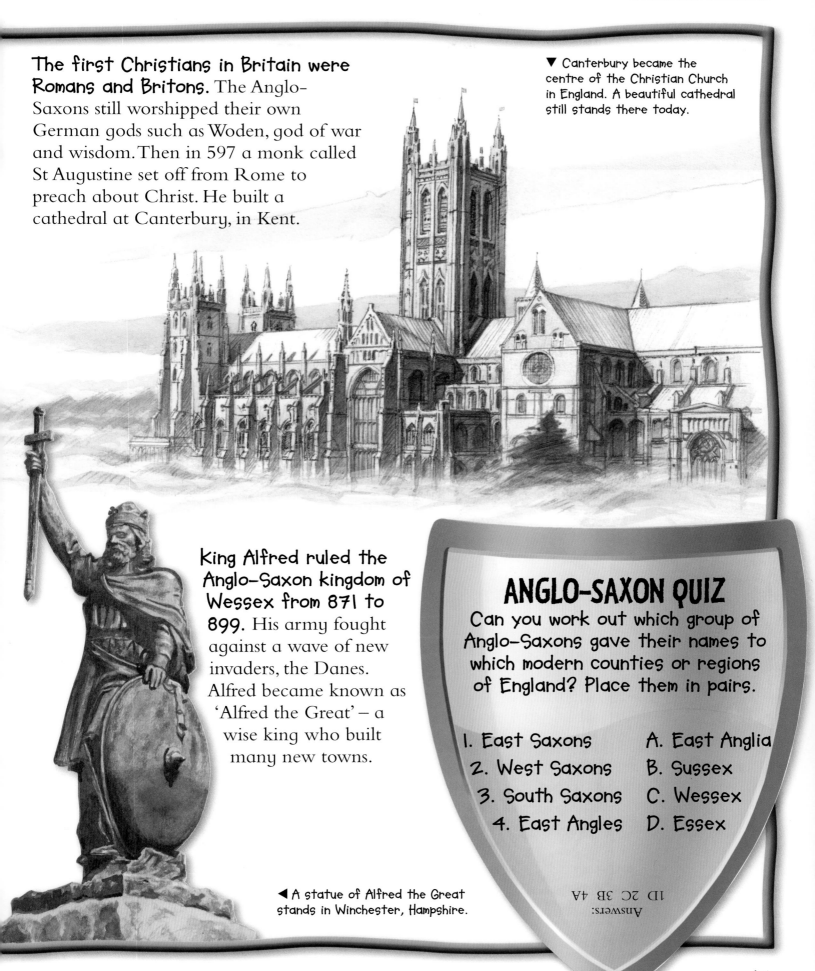

The first Christians in Britain were Romans and Britons. The Anglo-Saxons still worshipped their own German gods such as Woden, god of war and wisdom. Then in 597 a monk called St Augustine set off from Rome to preach about Christ. He built a cathedral at Canterbury, in Kent.

▼ Canterbury became the centre of the Christian Church in England. A beautiful cathedral still stands there today.

King Alfred ruled the Anglo-Saxon kingdom of Wessex from 871 to 899. His army fought against a wave of new invaders, the Danes. Alfred became known as 'Alfred the Great' – a wise king who built many new towns.

◀ A statue of Alfred the Great stands in Winchester, Hampshire.

ANGLO-SAXON QUIZ

Can you work out which group of Anglo-Saxons gave their names to which modern counties or regions of England? Place them in pairs.

1. East Saxons   A. East Anglia
2. West Saxons   B. Sussex
3. South Saxons   C. Wessex
4. East Angles   D. Essex

Answers: 1D 2C 3B 4A

The Irish

The Celtic-speaking people who lived in Ireland believed in the old Celtic gods. Then, in about 432, a British monk called St Patrick went to Ireland to preach the Christian faith. Over the next 200 years, monasteries were founded throughout Ireland. The monks made beautiful copies of the Bible by hand.

▲ About 1200 years ago, Irish monks made books by hand. They decorated their work with beautiful letters and pictures.

MAKE AN IRISH BROOCH

You will need:

scissors   stiff card   safety pin
gold and silver paint or pens

1. Cut out a circle and a long pin shape from stiff card. Glue them together.
2. Colour one side gold with paint or a pen. Decorate with patterns as shown below.
3. Tape a safety pin on the back at the widest part of the brooch so that it can be worn.

In the 700s and 800s, the Irish were some of the finest craftworkers in Europe. They made splendid brooches and cups of gold and silver, and were also famous for their stonework. The Irish were known as great storytellers, too.

In the 500s, an Irish monk called St Brendan is said to have sailed westwards to explore the lands around the Atlantic Ocean. Tales about his voyages tell of islands, whales and volcanoes.

Ireland was divided into separate kingdoms. Each ruler was supposed to recognize a High King as his chief, but the kings often quarrelled and fought with each other. In about 500, one northern group of Irish set up another kingdom called Dalriada, in western Scotland.

Brian Ború became High King of all Ireland in 1002. He fought many battles with other Irish kings. He also fought against invaders from Scandinavia, the Vikings. Brian Ború defeated all his enemies at Clontarf in 1014, but was murdered after the battle.

◀ The Battle of Clontarf marked the end of Viking power in Ireland.

The Vikings

The Vikings were pirates and raiders, traders, settlers, explorers and farmers. Some people called them Northmen or Danes, for their homeland was in Norway, Sweden and Denmark. Viking raiders began to attack the British Isles in 789 and were soon feared far and wide.

Viking longships were sleek, wooden vessels about 18 metres long. They had a single sail and could speed through the waves. The oars were manned by a crew of 30 or more. Ships like these carried Vikings far to the west, to Iceland, Greenland and North America.

▼ The Vikings were not just interested in raiding and stealing. They realized that the British Isles provided good farmland and safe areas for settlements.

Viking warriors attacked monasteries, villages and towns, carrying away treasure, cattle or slaves. They were armed with round shields, axes, swords and spears and wore helmets of leather or iron. Some spent the gold they robbed buying tunics made of tough iron rings, called mail.

Vikings fought against the Anglo-Saxons and soon controlled large areas of England. In 1016 England even had a Danish king called Cnut I. Vikings also ruled the Isle of Man and large areas of Scotland and Ireland.

In the 840s and 850s, Viking warriors began to settle in Britain and Ireland. They lived in villages and seaports and captured large towns such as York. They founded the city of Dublin in Ireland.

I DON'T BELIEVE IT!

Do you know what the word berserk means? To the Vikings it meant 'bearskin shirt', as worn by warriors who worked themselves up into a frenzy before going into battle. We still use the word today to describe someone who is violently angry.

The Welsh

The Anglo-Saxons did not settle in the land of the West Britons, although by 607 they had cut it off from the other Celtic lands to the north. They called this land Wales. In about 784, the Saxon king, Offa, built a massive wall of earth along the border as a defence against Welsh attacks. Offa's Dyke still stands today.

◄ Crosses on early Welsh churches were beautifully carved from stone.

► During the early Middle Ages, Wales was made up of several smaller kingdoms, each with its own ruler. These rulers were constantly fighting each other, trying to conquer the rest of Wales.

Wales and Cornwall had been centres of Christianity since Roman times. A Welsh priest called St David, who lived from 520 to 601, built new churches across the land.

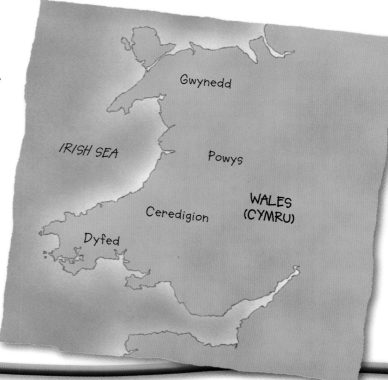

Wales was divided into several kingdoms. These included Gwynedd, Powys, Dyfed and Ceredigion. One ruler, Hywel the Good, ended up controlling most of Wales. He began to make new laws that were used in Wales for over 500 years. He died in 950.

▲ Welsh warriors patrolled the lands to the west of Offa's Dyke. They sometimes raided parts of England for cattle and slaves.

Llywelyn the Great came to rule Gwynedd in 1194. He was a wise and strong ruler. He married Joan, the daughter of King John of England, but the two men became bitter enemies.

◄ This stone head is said to be a sculpture of Llywelyn the Great.

Llywelyn ap Gruffudd united all of Wales under his rule. He fought a long war against the English and was killed near Cilmeri in 1282. The English now ruled Wales. King Edward I declared that in future the eldest son of the English king would be the Prince of Wales.

I DON'T BELIEVE IT!

Legend says that on 1 March 640 St David was at a battle between Christian soldiers from Wales and the non-Christian Saxons. St David told his men to wear leeks in their caps to show which side they were on. The leek is still an emblem of Wales today.

The Scots

In about 563 an Irish monk called Columcille, or Columba, founded a monastery on the Scottish island of Iona. He travelled all over Scotland and taught people about the Christian faith.

I DON'T BELIEVE IT!

In the days before printing, people had to copy books by hand. This was mostly done by monks. It is said that St Columba copied no fewer than 300 books himself!

Over the years the different parts of Scotland united as one country. The Scots and Picts joined together in 847 under the rule of Kenneth MacAlpin. By 1043 all the different peoples of Scotland belonged to the new kingdom as well, which was ruled by King Duncan I.

▶ Columba arrived on the Scottish island of Iona with a handful of companions. He converted many people to the Christian faith.

The Scottish kings had trouble controlling their border lands. Norwegians occupied islands and coasts in the north and west until the 1100s. After them, chieftains called the Lords of the Isles ruled much of the west. Along the southern border, war with England went on for hundreds of years.

Duncan I only ruled Scotland for six years. He was killed by a rival called Macbeth. Macbeth actually turned out to be a good king, but in 1057 Duncan's son, Malcolm, marched back into Scotland and killed Macbeth. Malcolm became king in 1058.

◄ Duncan I became king of Scotland in 1034. He was killed in battle by Macbeth.

► Margaret became Queen of Scotland aged 24. She brought many good changes to the country.

In 1070 Malcolm III was married in Dunfermline. His bride was an English lady who had been born in Hungary. Her name was Margaret. The new queen made the Scottish court a fine place. She founded many monasteries and the Church later made her a saint.

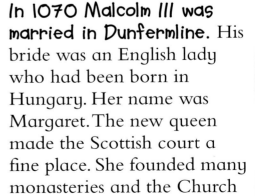

The Normans

An English king called Edward the Confessor died in 1066. Harold II became king after him, but no fewer than seven other people claimed that they should be king instead. One of these was William, Duke of Normandy. The Normans – Northmen – were descended from Vikings who had settled in France.

William crossed the English Channel with a fleet of ships. His army landed and met the English in a great battle near Hastings in Sussex. Axes crashed on shields, arrows whistled through the air, horses neighed. King Harold was killed and the Normans marched to London.

▶ The Norman army defeated the English at the Battle of Hastings in 1066.

William was crowned king of England in Westminster Abbey, London, on Christmas Day 1066. He built a stone fortress there, as part of the Tower of London. Soon William I controlled all England. He became known as William the Conqueror.

The Normans created the Domesday Book. In it they recorded the houses and lands in their new kingdom. People had to work for their new Norman lords and pay taxes. The Domesday Book helped the king keep track of everything.

Domesday Book

The Normans attacked and settled in parts of Wales. They also settled in the Lowlands of Scotland. By 1166 Norman knights were becoming involved in wars in Ireland and seizing land there, too.

During the 1100s the kings of England kept close links with France. They married into French families. King Henry II of England ruled an empire that stretched all the way to southwestern France.

TRUE OR FALSE?

1. The Normans were named after their first leader, Norman the Strong.

2. The kings of England spoke French after 1066.

3. William I became known as William the Wanderer.

Answers:
1. FALSE The word Normans comes from Northmen, meaning Vikings. 2. TRUE French was the language of the royal court until the 1300s. 3. FALSE He became known as William the Conqueror.

Castles and Knights

The Normans began to build castles in Britain. These were a type of fortress in which people lived. They helped to control areas that had been conquered. The first Norman castles were made of wood, but before long they were made with thick stone walls and had towers. Water-filled ditches called moats surrounded them. Castles were built in Britain for 400 years.

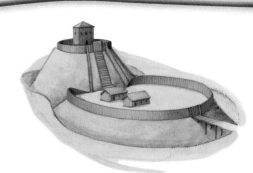

1000: a timber castle built on a mound

1150: a castle with a square stone tower, or keep

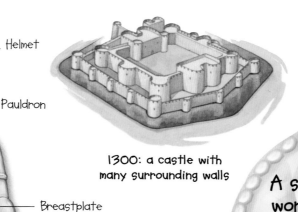

1300: a castle with many surrounding walls

Helmet

Pauldron

Breastplate

◀ By the 1400s knights wore armour of steel plates that covered the entire body. They no longer needed shields.

Tasset

Cuisse

I DON'T BELIEVE IT!

A suit of chain mail armour, as worn by a knight in the 1100s, weighed over 13 kilograms. Add to that weight the knight's great sword, axes and other weapons — and pity the poor warhorse!

From the Norman period onwards, the most important troops were mounted soldiers called knights. In battle, the knights were protected by armour. At first they wore chain mail. By the 1400s they wore plate armour that covered every part of the body, even the face.

Each noble family had its own badge called a coat-of-arms. This appeared on shields and flags and helped to show which knight was which during a battle. There were strict rules about the design of coats-of-arms, known as heraldry.

Knights liked to practise fighting in mock battles called tournaments. They showed off to the crowd and wore fancy armour. Even so, they often risked their lives.

▼ Knights engaging in foot combat wore heavy armour. Skill and speed were more important than strength.

In the great hall of the castle, lords and ladies feasted at grand banquets. There were many courses, with venison (deer meat), swan or goose, and all kinds of pies and puddings.

◄ A boar's head with all the trimmings was a popular dish at banquets.

29

Life in the Middle Ages

The king had power over everyone. If the nobles served him well, he gave them land and castles. Poor peasants had to work for the local lord, providing food and fighting services in return for land. It was a hard life and sometimes the peasants revolted (rebelled) in protest.

Lords sometimes revolted against the king, too. In England, lords forced King John to sign an agreement called Magna Carta in 1215. It said that even the king had to obey the laws of the land.

Towns were still quite small and were surrounded by high walls. The streets were narrow, muddy and smelly. Houses built of timber could catch fire all too easily.

All the Christians in western Europe now belonged to the Roman Church. Great stone cathedrals were built, soaring to the sky. People called pilgrims travelled far and wide to pray at holy sites, such as Canterbury Cathedral, in Kent.

In 1348 a terrible disease called the Black Death arrived in the British Isles. It was a plague that was spread by rat fleas biting people. This disease killed many millions of people right across Asia and Europe.

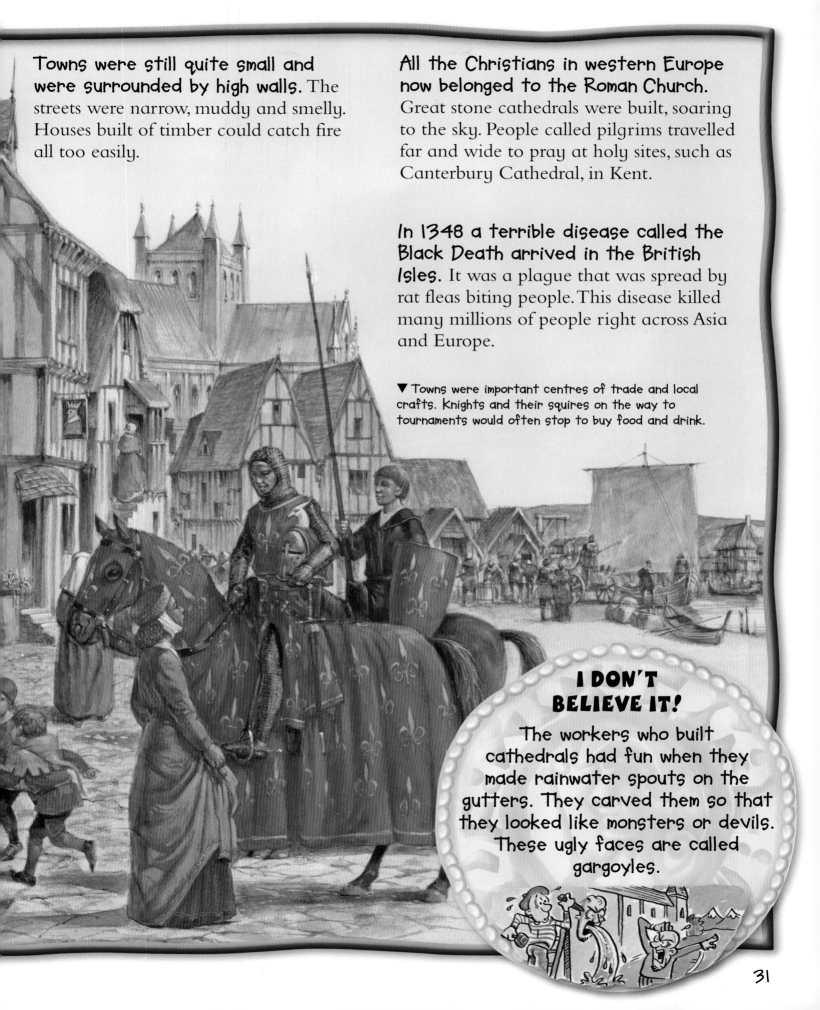

▼ Towns were important centres of trade and local crafts. Knights and their squires on the way to tournaments would often stop to buy food and drink.

I DON'T BELIEVE IT!

The workers who built cathedrals had fun when they made rainwater spouts on the gutters. They carved them so that they looked like monsters or devils. These ugly faces are called gargoyles.

Battles and wars

During the Middle Ages Christian knights from all over Europe began a terrible series of wars against people of other faiths. Most of these 'Crusades' were fought between 1096 and 1291 against Muslims in the Near East. King Richard I of England, known as *Coeur de Lion* or 'Lion Heart', led the Third Crusade in 1190.

The English and Scots were deadly enemies for many years. Scottish leaders included William Wallace and Robert Bruce. Bruce often despaired of victory. One day, whilst watching a spider try and try again to rebuild its web, he vowed to do the same. He defeated the English at Bannockburn in 1314.

I DON'T BELIEVE IT!

The first cannons either fizzled out or exploded with a great bang when fired. They sometimes did more harm to the soldiers firing them than they did to the enemy! In 1460 one exploding cannon even killed a king – James II of Scotland.

Christian knight

Saracen soldier

▲ During the Crusades, Christian knights battled with Muslim soldiers called Saracens.

The Welsh rose up against English rule in 1400. Their leader was called Owain Glyndwr. He made alliances with rebel English lords and with France. Welsh archers used the new longbow, a fearsome weapon, but the rising failed after 16 years of struggle.

The Hundred Years War did not last 100 years! It actually lasted longer – from 1337 to 1453. It was a series of wars between the English and the French. Henry V led the English to a great victory at Agincourt in 1415, but gradually England lost its lands in France.

English knight

Muslim archer

Scottish foot soldier

Welsh archer

▲ During the Middle Ages, soldiers wore different dress for battle. They also used various weapons. The English and Welsh both favoured the deadly longbow.

From 1455 to 1485, two families of English nobles fought for the throne in the Wars of the Roses. The badge of the House of Lancaster was a red rose, while the House of York had a white rose.

The red rose of Lancaster

The white rose of York

▶ Cannons such as this were hauled to battlefields during the Wars of the Roses.

Tudors and Stuarts

The Tudor family were of Welsh descent. They ruled England and Wales after 1485 and also controlled a small part of Ireland, around Dublin. The first Tudor king, Henry VII, united England under his rule. The Tudor rulers and nobles liked to live in fine palaces rather than draughty castles.

The Stuart family ruled Scotland. Their greatest king was James IV. He built a fleet of ships and fine palaces, too. Musicians and poets came to his court. James was killed fighting the English in 1513.

Henry VIII came to the English throne in 1509. People had great hopes of him being a good king, but as he grew older he became selfish and jealous. He married six times. Two of his wives were beheaded!

▶ Henry VIII was a good dancer and musician. His court was often the scene of extravagant royal balls. Henry was also an intelligent and capable king who was very interested in education and religion.

When Henry VIII tried to divorce his first wife, he quarrelled with the Pope in Rome. To get his divorce, Henry cut ties with Rome and made himself Head of the Church in England.

During the 1500s people were arguing about religion, in the British Isles and all over Europe. The Roman Catholics supported the Pope, but the Protestants wanted to break away from the Church in Rome. King Edward VI of England was a Protestant, but he died young. His sister, Mary I, was a Roman Catholic. In the 1550s she ordered many Protestants to be burnt alive when they refused to give up their faith.

TRUE OR FALSE?

1. Henry VIII had three of his wives beheaded.
2. Henry VIII liked to write pop songs.
3. Mary I of England was a Protestant.

Answers:
1. FALSE Two were beheaded.
2. TRUE He composed all kinds of music, including religious and popular songs. He loved dancing.
3. FALSE She was Catholic.

The Elizabethans

Elizabeth I, daughter of Henry VIII, came to the throne in 1558. She had her father's temper as well as his love of music, dancing and fine clothes. Unlike him, she never married. She was also a much wiser ruler than Henry. Elizabeth died in 1603, the last of the Tudors.

The English countryside was full of sheep in Tudor times. Merchants sold wool and cloth across Europe. Many parts of England became very wealthy.

Mary Stuart, Queen of Scots, fled to England in 1568. Scotland was going through troubled times. Although a cousin of Elizabeth, Mary was also a threat. In 1587 she was accused of plotting against Elizabeth and she was beheaded.

◄ Elizabeth I was greatly respected, and knew how to win public approval.

▲ The smaller, faster English ships defeated the mighty Spanish fleet, or Armada.

English seafarers were busy exploring. In 1577 to 1581 Sir Francis Drake sailed right round the world. By the 1600s, English people were settling along the coasts of North America. Their first settlement was called Virginia.

In 1588 Catholic Spain sent a fleet of ships (the Armada) to invade England. The Armada was attacked by English ships along the Channel and then scattered by storms.

TRUE OR FALSE?

1. The Spanish Armada was defeated by the English.

2. Mary Queen of Scots became Queen of England.

3. Elizabeth I was the daughter of Henry VII.

Answers:
1. TRUE
2. FALSE She was never crowned Queen.
3. FALSE She was the daughter of Henry VIII.

◀ Shakespeare's plays were first performed in the Globe Theatre during the 1600s.

In the 1590s and 1600s, theatres became very popular in London. People crowded into them to see the plays of William Shakespeare.

Roundheads and Cavaliers

Elizabeth I died without having had children. The throne passed to James VI of Scotland, son of Mary, Queen of Scots. James now became James I of England as well. James proved to be an intelligent king who wrote about the dangers of tobacco and introduced a new English translation of the Bible.

▲ Charles I lost the Civil War and was beheaded in 1649.

In 1605, soldiers searching the cellars of the Houses of Parliament discovered barrels of gunpowder. A Catholic called Guy Fawkes along with 12 other men was accused of plotting to blow up the king and Parliament. The failure of the plot has been celebrated every 5th November since then, with bonfires and fireworks.

▼ The leaders of the Gunpowder Plot were tortured before being put to death.

James' son, Charles I, forced people to pay unfair taxes. Members of Parliament were so angry that they went to war with the king. The king's soldiers were called Cavaliers and the soldiers of Parliament were called Roundheads. The Roundheads won and Charles had his head chopped off.

In 1653 Parliament handed over power to a soldier called Oliver Cromwell. He ruled as Lord Protector for five years. Cromwell was supported by extreme Protestants, called Puritans.

In 1660 Parliament decided to have a king again. The son of the old king (Charles I) became Charles II. The Puritans took life and religion seriously and did not like dancing or the theatre. But Charles II did – people started having fun again!

I DON'T BELIEVE IT!

When he was a student at Cambridge, Oliver Cromwell was more famous as a football player than as a politician. Football was a very rough game in those days, without the rules we know today.

▼ After the strict ways of the Puritans, people welcomed the more relaxed rule of Charles II.

Plague and fire

In 1665 the plague, or Black Death, returned to London. Thousands died in the first few months. Carts came round the streets to collect the dead. City folk fled to the countryside – taking their deadly germs with them.

In 1666 a spark from a fire set a bakery alight in Pudding Lane, London. The fire spread through the city for five whole days, destroying over 13,000 timber-framed houses and St Paul's Cathedral. The city was rebuilt in stone. A new cathedral was designed by Sir Christopher Wren.

▼ Rat fleas spread the Black Death, but people did not know this. Red crosses painted on doors told people that plague was present in a house.

▼ The Great Fire of London was made worse by strong winds. About 80 percent of the old city was destroyed.

When Charles II died in 1685, his brother became King James II of England (James VII of Scotland). James was a Catholic and the Protestants were angry. They threw him off the throne. Instead, they made his daughter Queen Mary II. Her Protestant husband William, who already ruled the Netherlands, became king. William III and Mary II ruled jointly.

Mary II

William III

The 1600s and 1700s were lawless times. Highwaymen lay in wait on lonely heaths and held up travellers' coaches. Pirates sailed the seas, attacking and robbing ships.

Queen Anne was the last of the Stuarts. She ruled from 1701 to 1714. In 1707 it was decided that England and Scotland should have the same parliament. England, Wales and Scotland were now a United Kingdom.

◄ Highwaymen preyed upon travellers, holding up coaches and stealing valuables. Some, such as Dick Turpin (1706 to 1739), even became well-known figures.

In the 1700s

After Queen Anne died, the throne passed to kings from the German state of Hanover. The first four were all called George. They ruled Britain in the 1700s. By now there were two political parties called the Whigs and the Tories. From 1721 there was a prime minister, too.

Clever new machines were invented to spin yarn and weave cloth. They used water power or steam power. Machinery also helped on the farm. Jethro Tull invented a machine for sowing seed.

▼ Canals and new ways of farming changed the landscape of Britain in the 1700s. In fact farming changed so much, this time became known as the Agricultural Revolution.

Canals were built across the British Isles in the 1700s. They were dug out by gangs of workers called navigators or navvies. It was easier to carry goods on barges than on bumpy, muddy, winding roads.

People called Jacobites wanted to bring back Stuart rule. Many lived in Scotland and that was where two rebellions started. James Edward Stuart (son of James VII of Scotland/II of England) was defeated in 1715. In 1745 his son, Bonnie Prince Charlie, almost succeeded, but he was forced to flee the country after a grim defeat at Culloden in 1746.

▼ At the Battle of Culloden, the English Redcoats easily defeated the Scottish Jacobites.

The British Redcoats carried guns with bayonets (long blades attached to the end of their guns) — they attacked the Jacobites without mercy

The Scottish Jacobites wore uniforms of plaid and carried swords and shields — but they were no match for the Redcoats

Jethro Tull's seed drill

1700s QUIZ

1. What was a navvie?
2. What did Jethro Tull invent?
3. When was the Declaration of Independence drawn up?

Answers:
1. Navigator — a canal worker. 2. The seed drill. 3. 1776.

In the 1700s British traders and soldiers were seizing land all over the world. They fought with France to gain control of Canada and India. However in 1776, Britain began to lose control of its American colonies when the Declaration of Independence was drawn up. This recognized the right of the United States to break from British rule.

In the 1800s

Britain was at war with France from 1791 to 1802 and from 1803 to 1815. The British admiral Horatio Nelson won a great sea battle near Trafalgar, Spain, in 1805. From now on Britain's navy ruled the seas. In 1815 Sir Arthur Wellesley, who became Duke of Wellington, defeated the French Emperor Napoleon on land, at Waterloo in Belgium.

George III was old and going mad, so in 1811 his son was made Prince Regent to rule in his place. This Regency period was a time of high fashion. Elegant new buildings and parks were built. In 1820 the prince became king as George IV. He ruled over a United Kingdom that had, since 1801, included Ireland.

I DON'T BELIEVE IT!

Bathing in the sea became very at fashionable at seaside towns. Shy people changed in huts on wheels, called bathing machines. These were hauled into the waves. Some people said seawater was so good for you that they drank it!

▼ The attempt by France to invade England failed at The Battle of Trafalgar. English cannons sank many French ships.

After 1804, new clanking, puffing monsters disturbed the peace of the countryside. Great Britain built the world's first railways. At first, steam locomotives were used in mines, but by the 1830s trains carried passengers.

The Victorians

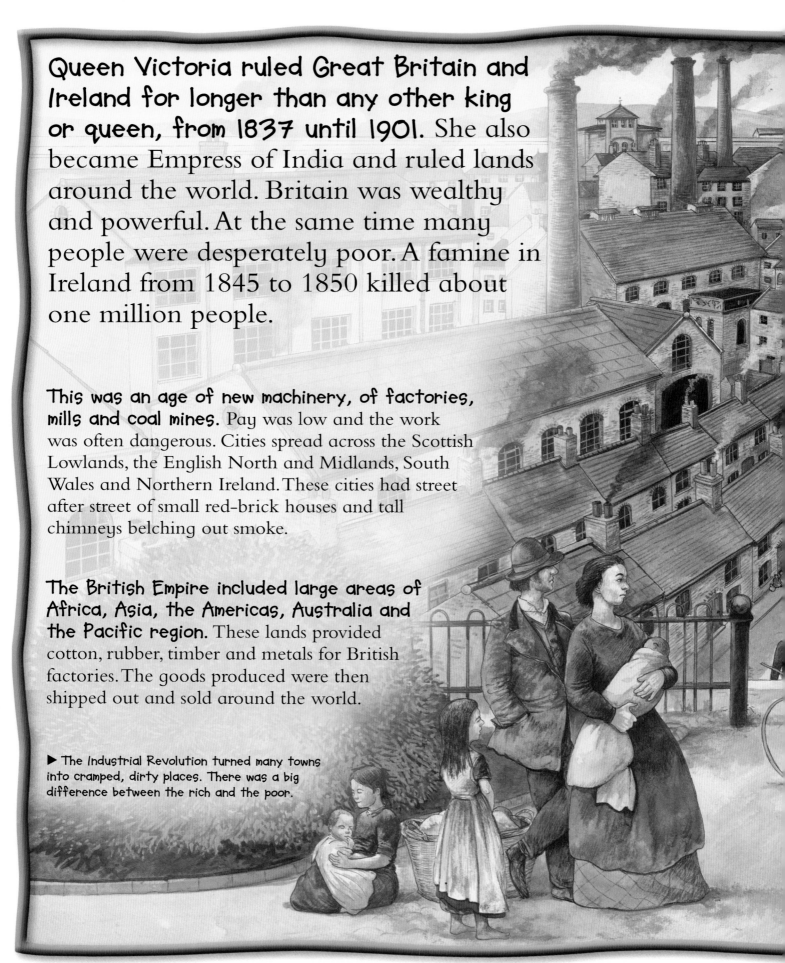

Queen Victoria ruled Great Britain and Ireland for longer than any other king or queen, from 1837 until 1901. She also became Empress of India and ruled lands around the world. Britain was wealthy and powerful. At the same time many people were desperately poor. A famine in Ireland from 1845 to 1850 killed about one million people.

This was an age of new machinery, of factories, mills and coal mines. Pay was low and the work was often dangerous. Cities spread across the Scottish Lowlands, the English North and Midlands, South Wales and Northern Ireland. These cities had street after street of small red-brick houses and tall chimneys belching out smoke.

The British Empire included large areas of Africa, Asia, the Americas, Australia and the Pacific region. These lands provided cotton, rubber, timber and metals for British factories. The goods produced were then shipped out and sold around the world.

▶ The Industrial Revolution turned many towns into cramped, dirty places. There was a big difference between the rich and the poor.

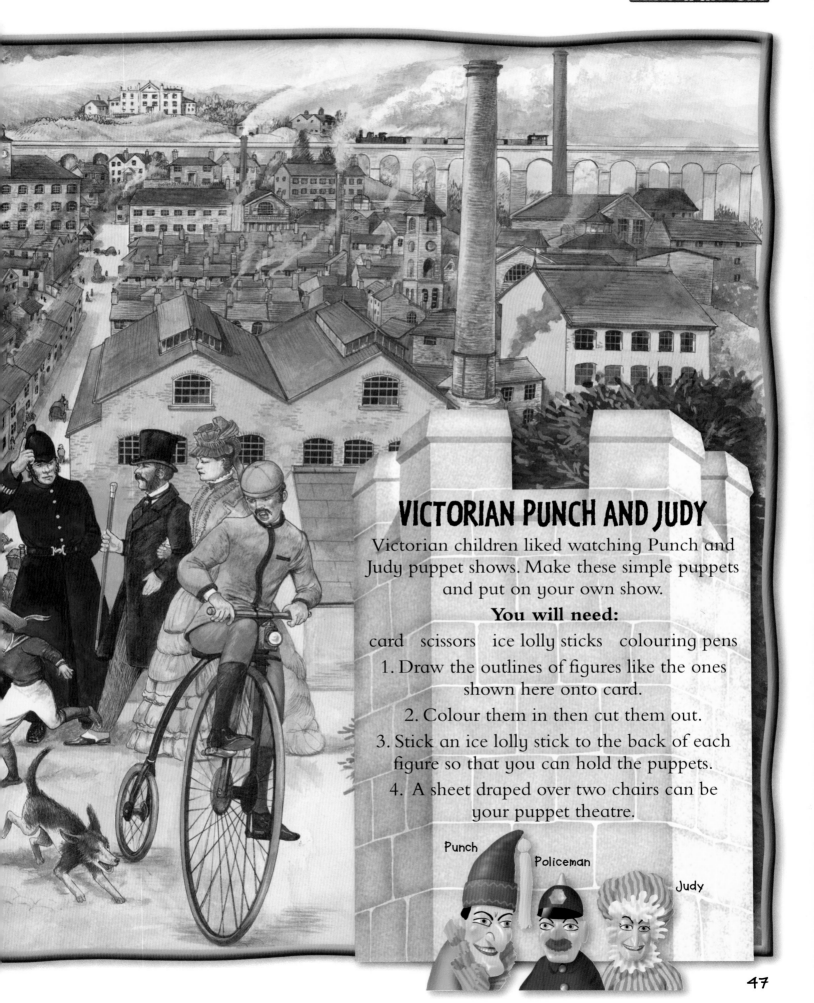

VICTORIAN PUNCH AND JUDY

Victorian children liked watching Punch and Judy puppet shows. Make these simple puppets and put on your own show.

You will need:

card   scissors   ice lolly sticks   colouring pens

1. Draw the outlines of figures like the ones shown here onto card.

2. Colour them in then cut them out.

3. Stick an ice lolly stick to the back of each figure so that you can hold the puppets.

4. A sheet draped over two chairs can be your puppet theatre.

Punch

Policeman

Judy

The modern age

From 1914 to 1918 the nightmare of war spread around the world. In Europe, soldiers fought in the mud, pounded by guns. New weapons were used such as tanks and poison gas. Ten million soldiers died in this First World War.

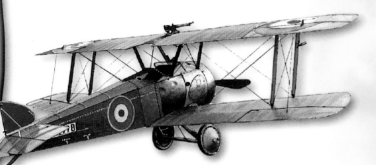

◄ During the First World War, the *Sopwith Camel* became the most famous British fighter plane.

In 1916 there was a rising against British rule in Ireland. In the years that followed, most of Ireland broke away from the United Kingdom and became a separate country. Across the old empire, other peoples were demanding their freedom.

In the early 1900s women were marching and protesting. Men had won the right to vote in elections. Now these women, or suffragettes, wanted to do the same. In 1918 women over 30 were given the right to vote, and in 1928 women were given the same voting terms as men.

The 1920s and 1930s were a fun time for those who had money. There were motor cars, new dance crazes and jazz records. But many people had no work – and no money. Men from the town of Jarrow walked all the way from the northeast of England to London to protest at their hardship.

◄ Hunger marchers left Jarrow for London to raise awareness of the terrible unemployment in the northeast.

The Second World War took place from 1939 to 1945. Britain and many other countries fought against brutal governments that had come to power in Germany, Italy and Japan. It was the worst war in history and millions of innocent people were killed. Here, British and German fighter planes chase each other during the Battle of Britain in 1940.

Inventions changed everyone's lives in the 20th century. This was the age of the car, the ocean liner, the aeroplane and the space rocket. It was the age of films, videos, telephones and computers. This was the modern age.

▲ The Battle of Britain began in the late summer of 1940. By October, the British had won this battle for the skies.

Queen Boudicca led a rebellion against Roman rule. Boudicca was wife of Prasutagus, king of a Celtic tribe who lived in eastern England. After his death, the Romans took over his kingdom. Boudicca was furious so, in AD 61, she led an army of Celtic tribes to attack Roman towns. After several Celtic successes, the Romans fought back and defeated the Celts. Rather than surrender, Boudicca took deadly poison and died. The Romans ruled most of Britain until AD 410 when they marched away leaving Celtic kings and queens in control. We know little about them. In fact, the most famous Celtic ruler – King Arthur – may never have existed!

▶ Queen Boudicca and her troops destroyed London. During her rebellion over 70,000 people were killed.

The first English Kings

King Alfred the Great ruled the Anglo-Saxon kingdom of Wessex from AD 871 to 899. At that time, Wessex was being attacked by Viking warriors. After several years, Alfred defeated them and gave his attention to building new towns. He encouraged scholars and was the very first English king to learn to read and write.

◀ This jewelled pointer was made for King Alfred and is decorated with his portrait. It was used to help follow lines of text on a page when reading.

King Offa ordered that a wall be built between his kingdom and Wales, to guard the border. King Offa, who ruled from AD 757 to 796, was king of Mercia, in the midlands. He is remembered for minting the first silver penny coins and for Offa's Dyke, much of which still stands today.

▶ This penny coin, made from real silver, is decorated with King Offa's portrait and his name.

Athelstan was the first king to rule all England. Until Athelstan's reign, AD 924 to 939, England was split into many warring kingdoms. Athelstan took control of them all. Then he led the English to victory against the Vikings and the Scots in AD 937.

Ethelred gave away England's gold.
Ethelred II became king in AD 978 when he was 12 years old, and died in 1016. Throughout his reign he had to defend England from the Vikings. Hoping to buy peace, he gave Viking armies *danegeld* – large sums of gold and silver coins. But each year they came back for more. For making this foolish decision, Ethelred became known as 'Ethelred the Unready' ('Ethelred-who-followed-bad-advice')!

King Edward the Confessor became a Christian saint. Edward ruled England from 1042 to 1066. His reign was peaceful but he meddled in international politics. To restore his reputation, his wife, Queen Emma, ordered that a book be written praising his life and devotion to God. When people read this, 100 years later, Edward was made a saint.

King Harold lost his eye – and his kingdom! Harold was the last Anglo-Saxon king of England, and ruled for just one year (1066). He led his army to Hastings to fight the Normans – invaders from France. When Harold was shot in the eye by an arrow, his men surrendered and a new Norman king, William the Conqueror, came to power.

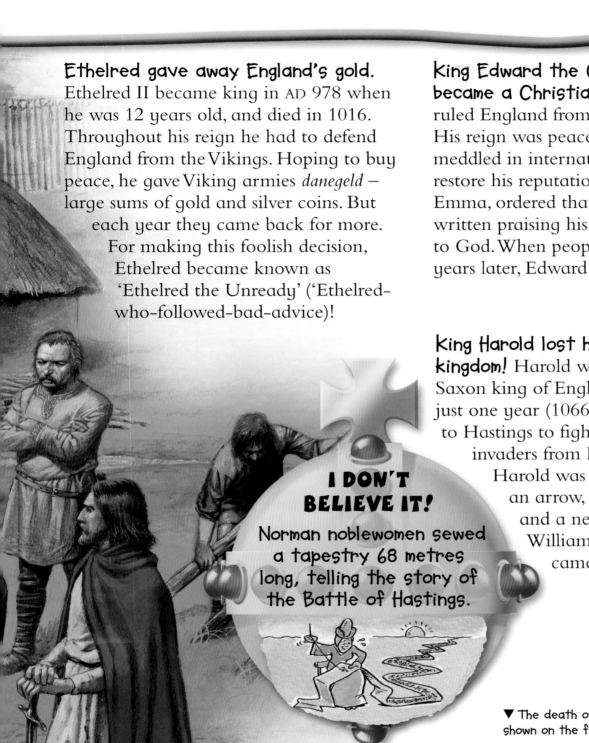

I DON'T BELIEVE IT!

Norman noblewomen sewed a tapestry 68 metres long, telling the story of the Battle of Hastings.

◀ After the Vikings invaded England, King Alfred and his soldiers hid in the Athelney Marshes, Somerset. In AD 886 the Vikings agreed to a peace treaty, which meant that southwest England was ruled by the Anglo-Saxons.

▼ The death of King Harold (centre) is shown on the famous Bayeux Tapestry.

Vikings in power

Cnut the Great was the most powerful Viking ruler. He was king of Denmark, Norway and England from 1016 to 1035. Although he was a harsh ruler, Cnut claimed to be a good Christian. To prove it, he staged a strange event on an English beach. He walked down to the sea, then commanded the waves to obey him. When they did not, he said, 'This proves that I am weak. Only God can control the sea.'

◄ King Cnut claimed to be weak, but in fact he ruled a large empire. He used his power as king to bring peace, which lasted until he died.

Erik Bloodaxe was a murderer – and was murdered. When his father died, he killed both his brothers so he could become king of Norway. To escape punishment he fled to England, where he ruled the Viking kingdom of York in AD 948, and again from AD 952 to 954. But enemies there forced him to leave and murdered him as he tried to escape.

Sven Forkbeard ruled England for just five weeks. Sven was king of Denmark from AD 998 to 1014. He led many Viking raids on Britain. Then in 1013 Sven invaded England, declared himself king and forced the English royal family to flee to France. Just five weeks later he fell ill and died.

Sigurd the Stout had a magic flag. Between AD 985 and 1014, Sigurd ruled many Scottish islands. He had a flag with a picture of a raven on it. Sigurd believed that whoever carried this flag was sure of victory for his army – but would die himself. In 1014 Sigurd carried his flag at the Battle of Clontarf, while fighting to win more land. He died – and his army lost the battle.

Thorfinn the Mighty – Viking and law-maker. Thorfinn was ruler of the Orkney Islands, off the north coast of Scotland, from 1020 to 1065. Since 900, the islands had been under Viking control. But this did not stop Scottish tribes from attacking. Thorfinn defended the islands against the Scots, then spent the rest of his reign planning new ways in which to govern and making new laws.

▲ After Sigurd the Stout lost the Battle of Clontarf, Viking power in Ireland began to decline.

ROYAL QUIZ

1. What kingdom was ruled by Eric Bloodaxe?

2. Who ruled England for just five weeks?

3. What was on the flag of Sigurd the Stout?

4. Did King Cnut stop the waves?

Viking king Sihtric Silkbeard was a warlord who wanted peace. He ruled Dublin, in Ireland, from AD 989 to 1036, but his lands were often attacked by Irish kings. To make peace, Sihtric married one of their daughters. Later, he gave up the kingship and went on two pilgrimages to the holy city of Rome. Unfortunately, he was murdered on his return journey in 1042.

Answers:
1. The Viking kingdom of York
2. Sven Forkbeard   3. A raven   4. No

New nations

Niall of the Nine Hostages was a pirate chief. Niall Noigiallach ruled the Irish kingdom of Tara from AD 445 to 452. He made many pirate raids along the west coast of Britain, to seize slaves and plunder. Legends say that Niall was the first high king of Ireland, and the ancestor of the powerful O'Neill family, who ruled Ireland for hundreds of years.

Brian Ború fought to drive Viking invaders away. King of Munster in Ireland from AD 976 to 1014, and also Ireland's high king, Brian won many victories. The most important was at Dublin in AD 999, when Brian drove Viking settlers out of the city. But Vikings returned and befriended Brian's Irish enemies. He was killed in the fighting that followed.

► Pirate ships had shallow hulls so that raiders could land easily on rocky shores.

Rhodri Mawr (the Great) ruled Gwynedd, in north Wales, from AD 844 to 878. He fought to defend his kingdom and win land, riches and power. Rhodri also expanded his kingdom by marrying Princess Angharad, daughter of the ruler of the Welsh kingdom of Ceredigion. He took over her father's lands and became the first king to rule almost all of Wales.

No one knows where Cinead (Kenneth) MacAlpine came from. But he soon became famous throughout Scotland for his brave – but bloodthirsty – fighting skills. At that time the Scots and Picts ruled two separate kingdoms in Scotland. Cinead conquered both and became the first king of Scotland, from AD 840 to 858.

▶ Viking soldiers probably helped Cinead MacAlpine to become king of Scotland.

People remember Macbeth as the murderous, haunted hero of a play written by William Shakespeare. But Macbeth was a real king who ruled Scotland from 1040 to 1057. Macbeth's life was certainly violent. To win power, he burned his chief rival alive, married his widow, then fought and killed another Scottish noble who wanted to be king. Once in power, Macbeth ruled wisely, defending Scotland from invasions and protecting the Church.

English – Keep out

Llywelyn the Great demanded loyalty. Prince of Gwynedd (North Wales) from 1194 to 1240, Llywelyn created a government to unite Wales and introduced new ways of ruling. He also gave orders for traditional laws to be gathered and written down and collected taxes in money – rather than in cattle or corn!

▲ Llywelyn the Great fought against rival princes and forced them to swear loyalty to him and his son.

Llywelyn ap Gruffudd (the Last) was prince of Wales from 1246 to 1282. His reign began gloriously, as he led the Welsh to fight against English invaders. But it ended in disaster. English king Edward I sent soldiers to kill Llywelyn. They cut off his head and took it to London where it was crowned with ivy and put on a spiked pole. Llywelyn was the last Welsh prince to rule Wales.

◄ While planning his next battle against King Edward, Llywelyn ap Gruffudd was killed by English soldiers.

One king's protector turned into his ruler. From 1132 to 1166, Dairmait Mac Murchadha (Dermot Mac Murrough) was king of Leinster, in Ireland. Then his enemies chased him to England, where he sought refuge with Henry II. Dermot returned to Ireland in 1169 and Henry sent soldiers to protect his kingdom. At first Dermot welcomed them, but they soon took over his lands. For the next 800 years, and more, English kings claimed the right to rule Ireland.

Scottish nobleman Robert Bruce lived at a time when English kings were trying to conquer Scotland and Wales. The Scots crowned Bruce king in 1306. At first his armies were defeated, but he would not give in. A story tells how, while hiding in a cave, Bruce watched a spider making efforts to repair its web. This inspired him to go on fighting, and the English finally recognized Scotland's independence in 1328.

▶ Robert Bruce became one of Scotland's national heroes, along with other fighters for independence, such as 'Braveheart' William Wallace (executed 1305).

I DON'T BELIEVE IT!

James I of Scotland was murdered in a sewer. He was escaping enemies through a drainpipe but became stuck because he was too fat!

Kings of Scotland

Alexander III (ruled 1249 to 1286) was a successful king, winning new lands and allies for Scotland. But he had no son to rule after him, so he married a young wife. He was so keen to see her one night that he set out on horseback. But his horse tripped in the dark and the king fell over a cliff and was killed.

James II was killed by his own gun. James (ruled 1437 to 1460) was interested in the latest battle technology. Unfortunately he was killed by one of his own cannons, which exploded while he was watching it being fired.

The tough ruler of Scotland from 1460 to 1488, James III made many enemies. One lord kidnapped him, another locked him in prison, and his own son helped plan the plot that finally killed him. James was stabbed to death as he slept in a cottage, where he was sheltering after a battle.

James IV was a soldier, scholar and sportsman. He ruled from 1488 to 1513 and won fame as a fighter. He was also intelligent, sensible and fond of sport (especially jousting). James built palaces, helped schools and universities, and licensed Scotland's first printing press. He died at the Battle of Flodden, a defeat that marked the end of Scotland's power as an independent country.

▼ James IV and leading Scottish nobles were killed by the English army at the Battle of Flodden in 1513.

James IV

MAKE SOME FLAGS

Try making these English and Scottish flags

You will need:

scissors   old sheet   pencil
fabric paint   bamboo canes
sticky tape

1. Cut out a rectangle of cloth from the sheet.

2. In pencil mark out your chosen design.

3. Use fabric paint to colour the flags, like the designs below.

4. Attach the flags to the bamboo cane with sticky tape.

Scotland

England

Norman conquerors

William the Conqueror changed England's laws — and the English language! William was king of England from 1066 to 1087. Born in France, he became Duke of Normandy at the age of eight. When Edward the Confessor died, William claimed the English throne. He invaded, and killed king Harold at the Battle of Hastings in 1066. William ordered a survey (the Domesday Book) of the land so he could tax it. He introduced French laws and many words such as 'baby' and 'robe'.

William the Conqueror brought castles to Britain by sea. His soldiers made them in sections, from wood, before they invaded in 1066 and loaded them on to their warships. When the Normans arrived in England, they put the castles together and used them as army bases.

Was William II shot by a friend or an enemy? The second son of William the Conqueror, William Rufus, ruled England from 1087 to 1100. He died, shot by an arrow, while hunting. No one knows who fired the lethal shot.

Henry I, the third son of William the Conqueror, was well educated. He is only the second English king whom we know for certain could read and write. He became king in 1100 but had to fight his brothers to keep power. Henry won, and ruled for 35 years.

Henry I left no son to rule after him. When Henry died in 1135, Stephen, his nephew, claimed the right to be king. But Henry's daughter, Matilda, was furious. Henry had promised that she would be queen. In 1141 Matilda raised an army to fight Stephen. Although Stephen won he was forced to agree to Matilda's eldest son becoming king after him.

▲ The Normans built simple 'motte and bailey' castles. Each had a wooden tower, standing on a tall earth mound called a 'motte', in Norman French, surrounded by a strong wooden fence called a 'bailey'.

I DON'T BELIEVE IT!
Henry I died from eating too many eels!

Empress Matilda was the daughter of Henry I – and she was as fierce as her father. Matilda was brave, too. After she was captured in the war against Stephen, she escaped from Oxford Castle through thick snowdrifts, disguised in a white cloak.

Quarrelsome Kings

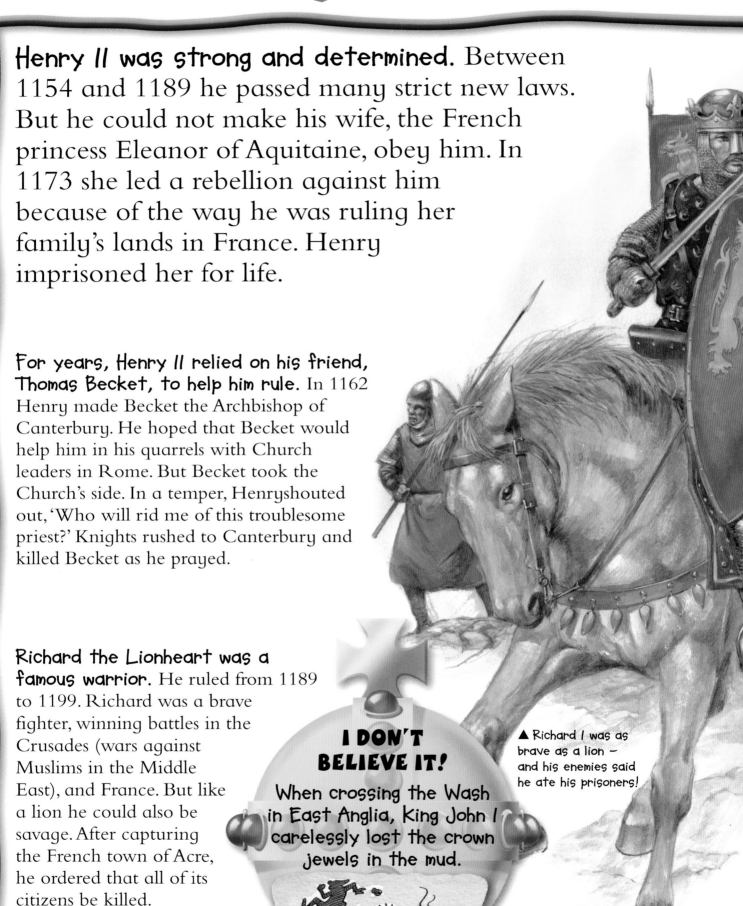

Henry II was strong and determined. Between 1154 and 1189 he passed many strict new laws. But he could not make his wife, the French princess Eleanor of Aquitaine, obey him. In 1173 she led a rebellion against him because of the way he was ruling her family's lands in France. Henry imprisoned her for life.

For years, Henry II relied on his friend, Thomas Becket, to help him rule. In 1162 Henry made Becket the Archbishop of Canterbury. He hoped that Becket would help him in his quarrels with Church leaders in Rome. But Becket took the Church's side. In a temper, Henryshouted out, 'Who will rid me of this troublesome priest?' Knights rushed to Canterbury and killed Becket as he prayed.

Richard the Lionheart was a famous warrior. He ruled from 1189 to 1199. Richard was a brave fighter, winning battles in the Crusades (wars against Muslims in the Middle East), and France. But like a lion he could also be savage. After capturing the French town of Acre, he ordered that all of its citizens be killed.

I DON'T BELIEVE IT!

When crossing the Wash in East Anglia, King John I carelessly lost the crown jewels in the mud.

▲ Richard I was as brave as a lion — and his enemies said he ate his prisoners!

Henry III was England's longest-reigning king. After coming to the throne in 1216 Henry ruled for 56 years, until 1272. But Henry's reign was not popular. He made people poor by collecting taxes to pay for wars in France. Yet his armies lost most of the battles.

► Henry III's beautiful tomb still survives and is admired by visitors at Westminster Abbey today.

Henry III was devoted to his family — and to his pets. He owned Britain's first zoo. Henry spent the last years of his reign planning a new cathedral (Westminster Abbey in London), where he was buried in a beautiful tomb.

King John I was an unpopular ruler. During his reign (1199 to 1216) he faced many problems. In 1215, nobles angry with his rule forced him to issue Magna Carta. This document guaranteed people basic legal rights. But John refused to follow it and his reign ended in civil war.

▼ Nobles forced King John to sign Magna Carta. It stated that even kings had to obey the law.

Edward I tried to make his kingdom bigger and better. King of England from 1272 to 1307, Edward made many new laws. He also wanted to win new lands. By 1284 he had conquered Wales and built splendid castles there to control it. He never managed to conquer Scotland although he fought many battles against Scottish soldiers.

Edward I was England's tallest – and angriest – king! 'Longshanks' (long-legs) Edward measured over two metres tall, and was one of the tallest men in Britain. He was also one of the most hot-tempered. He once tore out his son's hair in a fury, and broke his daughter's coronet. In 1290 he quarrelled with Jewish businessmen over money and religion and forced Jewish people to leave Britain.

I DON'T BELIEVE IT!

When Edward I was stabbed with a poisoned dagger, people say his wife saved him by sucking out the poison.

▼ Edward I's Welsh castles were designed with strong 'curtain' walls and tall look-out towers. Many were also surrounded by deep moats filled with water.

Edward II married a 'she-wolf'! That's what he called his wife, Isabella. She was the daughter of the king of France. As king (he ruled from 1307 to 1327) Edward was foolish and cruel. By 1325, Isabella could stand no more and she ran away to France.

▲ Edward III's armies won victories against France at Crécy (1346) and Poitiers (1356). They were led by his eldest son, who was nicknamed the 'Black Prince'.

Edward III claimed to be king of France. Since 1066, kings of England had owned lands in France. Edward III (king of England and Wales from 1327 to 1377) also claimed he was the rightful French king. This led to the Hundred Years War between England and France.

▼ Young Richard won praise for his bravery, but as he grew older he became proud and very unpopular.

Edward III lived in terrible times. In 1348 a disease called the Black Death, or the plague, reached England. Victims developed a cough, high fever and black boils. Almost half the people in England died. At the time, no one knew what caused the Black Death. Today, we know that it was spread by rat fleas.

Richard II was a teenage king. He ruled from 1377 to 1399. At the age of 14 he faced attack from mobs of workers. They had marched on London to protest about taxes, low wages and unfair laws. Bravely, Richard talked to the protesters and promised to help them – then his guards seized their leaders and killed them!

The Henrys

Henry IV was not the lawful heir to the throne. After a career as a soldier, Henry was hungry for power. In 1399 his soldiers placed Richard II in prison, where he died and Henry became king. He killed many others who questioned his right to the throne. Then he developed a skin disease, which killed him in 1413. People said it was punishment from God for his misdeeds.

ROYAL QUIZ

1. Which Henry beat the French at Agincourt?
2. Who died of a terrible skin disease?
3. Which king signed Magna Carta?
4. The Hundred Years War was fought between which countries?

Answers:
1. Henry V in 1415 2. Henry IV in 1413 3. John I in 1215
4. France and England

Henry V could not wait to be king. Henry ruled from 1413 to 1422. People said he was so eager to be king that he took the crown from his dying father's head and tried it on! But the king of France made fun of Henry. He sent him a present of tennis balls! This was his way of saying that Henry should stay at home and play, rather than try to be king.

Henry V won a famous victory in the Hundred Years War. In 1415 his army defeated the French knights at the Battle of Agincourt. Crowds welcomed Henry home as he rode through the streets of London, which were decorated with huge figures of heroes and giants.

◄ Henry V died aged 35 from a stomach illness caught in an army camp.

Henry VI became king in 1421, aged just nine months old. As he grew up he was peaceful and religious but suffered from a mental illness. Without a strong king, rival nobles tried to seize power. During the fighting Henry's only son was killed and Henry was put in prison, where he died in 1471.

The battles fought between rival nobles during Henry VI's reign were known as the 'Wars of the Roses'. The nobles owed loyalty to two families – the Lancasters and the Yorks – who were enemies. Each family used a rose as a badge to identify its soldiers – the Lancaster rose was red and the York rose was white.

▼ French knights were massacred by Henry V's longbowmen as they charged downhill at the Battle of Agincourt.

Killers and Kidnappers

Edward IV was a brave fighter, a clever army commander and a good politician. He became king in 1461. Edward liked food, drink and pretty women. He was also ruthless in his search for power and he gave orders for Henry VI to be murdered. When he suspected his brother of plotting against him, he ordered him to be drowned. Edward died in 1483.

▶ Edward IV won his first battle in 1416 when he was 18. Nobles fighting with him against Henry VI agreed he should be the next king.

Edward IV's wife was no lady! Few people dared disobey Edward – except Elizabeth Woodville. Edward wanted her to be his girlfriend but she refused. She insisted that he marry her, and to the royal family's horror, he agreed. Her family wanted to share in the king's riches.

▲ Elizabeth Woodville, Edward IV's queen, had five brothers and seven sisters – all greedy for wealth and power.

Prince Edward was 13 when his father, Edward IV, died in 1483. A few weeks later, Edward was kidnapped by his uncle, Richard of York, and locked in the Tower of London with his brother. The two 'Princes in the Tower' were never seen in public again and their uncle became king as Richard III. People thought that Richard had murdered them. In 1674 the skeletons of two boys were found buried in the Tower. Possibly, they were the remains of the princes.

Richard III was the last English king to die in battle. Richard became king in 1483. Just two years after seizing power, he was killed at the Battle of Bosworth Field. He insisted on wearing his crown with his armour. This made him an easy target for enemy soldiers.

MAKE A ROYAL CROWN

You will need:

tape measure   pencil   gold or silver card
ruler   scissors   glue   paintbrush
scraps of coloured paper

1. Use the tape measure to calculate the distance around your head.
2. Draw a crown shape in pencil on the back of the card. Make the distance A to B slightly more than the distance around your head. Make the distance B to C 10 centimetres.
3. Cut out the crown. Glue both ends together to make a circle. Leave to dry.
4. Decorate your crown with jewels cut from scraps of coloured paper.

The distance B to C (10 centimetres) is the height of the crown

The distance A to B is the distance measured around your head

Richard III is a hero to some people today. They believe that he was a good king and that the bad stories about him were invented by a historian, Sir Thomas More. He worked for the Tudors, who ruled after Richard.

◀ Richard III died at the Battle of Bosworth Field after ruling for just two years.

The Tudors

Henry VII

Henry VII founded a new ruling family. Henry Tudor was the son of a Welsh lord and an English noblewoman. He had a weak claim to be king but he won power by killing Richard III in battle in 1485. He brought peace to England, and an end to the Wars of the Roses. When he died in 1509, England was richer and calmer than it had been for hundreds of years.

1. Catherine of Aragon married Henry in 1509

2. Anne Boleyn married Henry in 1533 – she was beheaded in 1536

Henry VIII had six wives, but not at the same time! Henry ruled from 1509 to 1547 and lived happily with his first wife, Catherine of Aragon, for almost 20 years. But they didn't have a son and Henry was desperate for an heir. So he divorced Catherine in 1533 and married again – and again and again! Of the six wives Henry married, only one, Jane Seymour, gave him a son.

▶ As a young man, Henry VIII was fit, handsome and keen on music and sport. But as he became older he grew fat, unhealthy and very bad-tempered.

72

Henry VIII led a religious revolution. He defended the Catholic Church against complaints from Protestant reformers. Then he found himself quarrelling with the Catholic Church because it would not give him a divorce from his first wife. To get his divorce, Henry set up a break-away Church with himself as the head. It became known as the Church of England. Henry also shut down communities of monks and nuns who remained loyal to the Catholic Church – and took their money and lands for himself.

REMEMBERING RHYME

This rhyme helps you to remember the fate of Henry VIII's six wives:

divorced, beheaded, died, divorced, beheaded, survived

3. Jane Seymour married Henry in 1536 and died in 1537

4. Anne of Cleves married Henry in 1540 and was divorced just six months later

5. Catherine Howard married Henry in 1540 – and was beheaded a year later

6. Catherine Parr married Henry in 1543 – and survived her husband by one year

Henry VIII set up the first modern navy. He was the first king to realize that England, an island, needed a proper navy. So he paid for 20 new ships, all specially designed for war, and for full-time captains to command them. The most famous was the splendid *Mary Rose*, which sank as she left harbour in 1545.

▼ The *Mary Rose* sank after water poured though the gun-ports (holes for firing cannon) that had been cut into her hull.

Edward VI never had a chance to rule. He became king in 1547 at the age of nine when his father, Henry VIII, died. But his uncles ran the country for him and did not want to hand over power. Then Edward fell ill and died in 1553 aged just 16.

◀ Edward VI was a serious, clever boy who liked studying.

Lady Jane Grey was queen for just nine days. When Edward VI died in 1553, Jane's father-in-law, the Duke of Northumberland, wanted to run the country. So he tried to make Jane queen. But Mary Tudor had a better claim to the throne. Her supporters marched to London, imprisoned Jane and executed the Duke. Jane was executed a few months later.

▲ Lady Jane Grey was beheaded to stop powerful people trying to make her queen for a second time.

Philip II

Mary I was the first woman to rule England on her own. She was Henry VIII's eldest child but the law said her younger brother Edward should rule before her – because he was a boy. After Edward died – and after Lady Jane was put in prison – Mary ruled England from 1553 to 1558. Mary was popular, but her husband, King Philip II of Spain, was not. Mary died without having children.

Mary I

▼ Many Tudor people believed that religion was worth dying for. Some people faced death rather than change their beliefs.

Mary I killed hundreds of people — because she thought it was the right thing to do. Mary was a devout Catholic. She thought that Protestant religious ideas were wicked and wrong and believed it was her duty to make England Catholic again. So she threatened to execute all Protestants who would not give up their beliefs — by burning them alive.

I DON'T BELIEVE IT!

Almost 300 people died for their faith during Mary Tudor's reign and she became known as Bloody Mary.

Queens, cousins – and rivals

Soon after she came to power in 1558, Elizabeth I decided not to marry. This was partly because of her own experience – her mother had been executed by order of her father, Henry VIII. But it was also for political reasons. She did not want to share her power with any English nobleman or foreign prince. When Elizabeth died in 1603, the Tudor line came to an end.

Elizabeth claimed to have 'the heart and stomach of a king'. When England was attacked by the Spanish Armada (battle fleet) in 1588, Elizabeth rode on a white horse to meet troops waiting to fight the invaders. She made a rousing speech and said that she was not as strong as a king, but she was just as brave and determined.

Elizabeth had her own personal pirate. He was Sir Francis Drake, a brilliant sailor who was the first Englishman to sail around the world. But he also made many pirate attacks, especially on ships carrying treasure back to Spain. Elizabeth pretended not to know about them but secretly encouraged Drake – then demanded a share of his pirate loot when he returned home!

I DON'T BELIEVE IT!

Elizabeth I sent priests to prison for wearing the wrong clothes!

▲ Elizabeth knighted Drake in 1581 on board the *Golden Hind*.

Mary Queen of Scots became queen in 1542, at just six days old. She grew up in France and married the French king. When he died in 1561 she returned to Scotland. Mary was an unsuccessful queen – the Scots hated her – and a disastrous wife. She plotted to kill her second husband, Englishman Henry Darnley – then ran off with the man who murdered him! The Scots turned Mary off the throne in 1567 and her son, James VI, became king.

Mary Queen of Scots ran away to England and asked her cousin, Elizabeth I, to shelter her. Elizabeth did not trust Mary and put her in prison for almost 20 years. Even there, Mary did not stop plotting against Elizabeth. She made plans with Catholics in England and Europe who wanted her to be queen. Finally Elizabeth could stand no more and she had Mary executed in 1587.

▶ A Catholic plot was uncovered and Mary was accused of being involved. She was beheaded at Fotheringay Castle in February 1587.

When a king lost his head

James VI and James I were the same man. After Elizabeth I died, her distant cousin, James Stuart, became king of England and Wales. He was already king of Scotland, the sixth Scottish king called James, but the first in England with that name. He ruled each country separately – England and Scotland were not one united kingdom until 1707.

James was the first anti-smoking campaigner. Tobacco, which originated in America, was first brought to Europe in the late 16th century. It soon became popular but James hated it! He wrote a book describing smoking as 'a custom loathsome to the eye, hateful to the nose, harmful to the brain, and dangerous to the lungs'.

James I was called 'the wisest fool'. He was intelligent and ruled wisely, on the whole, from 1603 to 1625. But he did not look clever! His clothes were untidy and he slobbered and snivelled. He was also foolishly fond of several very silly friends.

Charles I believed he had a divine right to rule. King Charles (ruled 1625 to 1649) thought that kings were chosen by God. They had a divine (holy) right to lead armies and make laws. Anyone who disagreed with them was sinful. Not surprisingly, many of Charles's subjects did not share his views!

▶ A Cavalier (royalist) soldier (left) and a Roundhead soldier from Parliament's army.

◀ In 1653, Oliver Cromwell became Lord Protector. Here, Bible in hand, he makes a rousing speech to his Roundhead troops. Both sides in the English Civil War believed that they were fighting for God, and prayed that He would bring them victory.

King Charles was a devoted husband and father and he was keen on the arts. But he was not a very good king. He quarrelled so badly with Parliament about religion and taxes that he provoked a Civil War between Roundheads (supporters of Parliament) and Cavaliers (the royal family's supporters). After six years of fighting, from 1642 to 1648, Charles was put on trial, found guilty and executed.

For eleven years, England (and Scotland and Wales) had no king. At first, a Council of State ran the country. But in 1653 Parliament chose the commander of the Roundheads, Oliver Cromwell, to rule as Lord Protector. Cromwell was strict, solemn and deeply religious. He tried to bring peace. After his death in 1658 his son Richard ruled – badly. Parliament decided it was time for another king.

I DON'T BELIEVE IT!

Oliver Cromwell asked for his portrait to be painted showing him exactly as he was – even if it wasn't very attractive!

Charles II escaped to France when his father, Charles I, was killed. In 1660, he came back to England to be crowned king. Many people welcomed him. Like them, he wanted peace and religious toleration at home. Charles II enjoyed art, music, dancing and the theatre – and he had many girlfriends.

Charles was interested in all the latest scientific ideas. He set up a new Royal Observatory at Greenwich in south London, and appointed top astronomers to work there. Sadly, science killed him. His doctors gave him poisonous medicines and he died in 1685.

▲ Witty, pleasure-loving Charles II was nicknamed 'the merry monarch'.

Did James II try to pass off someone else's son as his own? When Charles died, his brother James became king. But James wanted to make England Catholic again. He had a daughter who had been brought up as a Protestant. Suddenly, and surprisingly, in 1688 James announced that his queen had given birth to a boy who would be England's next Catholic king. People accused James of smuggling a baby into the queen's bedroom. Parliament acted quickly – and turned James off the throne in 1688.

ROYAL QUIZ

1. What did Charles II set up at Greenwich?

2. Who was king after Charles II?

3. Who was Mary II's husband?

4. How did William III die?

Answers:
1. The Royal Observatory 2. James II
3. William of Orange
4. He was thrown off his horse when it tripped on a molehill

Mary II was the daughter of King James II. Unlike him, she was a Protestant, along with her husband, Dutch prince William of Orange. After sending James II into exile, Parliament asked Mary to be queen. She agreed, so long as her husband could be king as William III. They were crowned as joint monarchs in 1689.

▶ In 1688, Mary II and her husband William were called back to Britain from the Netherlands to become king and queen.

▶ Queen Anne warned her ministers not to bully her into making decisions, just because she was a woman.

William III was killed by a mole! One morning in 1702, William's horse tripped over a molehill and the king was thrown off. He died a few days later. Supporters of James II were delighted and hoped that James' son, James Edward Stuart, would become king. They praised the mole which had dug the molehill, calling him 'the little gentleman in black velvet'.

Queen Anne united two kingdoms. Anne was the younger sister of Mary II. Her private life was tragic. She became pregnant 17 times, but all her babies were either born dead, or died very young. But her reign (1702 to 1714) saw major changes in Britain. Parliament passed laws uniting England and Scotland and banning anyone but a Protestant from being the British king or queen.

Rulers from Germany

George I never learned English! He preferred to speak German or French. He also preferred living in Germany, where he ruled Hanover and other states as well England. George was the great-grandson of King James VI and I. He had the best claim to rule England after Queen Anne died without leaving any heirs.

▲ This coin was made in memory of the coronation of George I in 1714.

▼ George I was king of England, Wales and Scotland from 1714 to 1727.

George I kept his wife in prison. George's wife, Sophia Dorothea, was lonely. When she made friends with a handsome nobleman, George was furious. He locked Sophia away in a German castle and refused to tell his children what had happened to their mother. They never forgave him.

I DON'T BELIEVE IT!

George II died while visiting the closet (royal lavatory). He collapsed there from a heart attack.

George II was the last English king to ride into battle — and he fell off his horse! This happened in 1743 at the Battle of Dettingen. The British army won many victories during George's reign (1727 to 1760), conquering new lands in Canada and India and stopping rebellions in Scotland.

James Edward Stuart was the only surviving son of King James II. He lived in France, but claimed to be the rightful English and Scottish king. The British Parliament disagreed. They called James 'the Old Pretender'. In 1715 James invaded Scotland but he was forced out by George II's soldiers. He spent the rest of his life in Rome.

▲ Scottish highlanders, known as Jacobites, fought for James Edward Stuart and his son, Charlie.

Bonnie Prince Charlie was called 'the Young Pretender'. Charlie, who lived from 1720 to 1788, was the son of James Edward Stuart. He also claimed the right to be king. When he invaded Scotland in 1745 his attack went well. His army marched towards London but was forced to retreat by English soldiers. The next year, all that was left of Charlie's army was massacred at the Battle of Culloden, near Inverness.

▼ The Battle of Culloden in 1746 was the last major battle fought on British soil. Afterwards, Bonnie Prince Charlie spent many months in hiding, until Jacobite heroine, Flora MacDonald helped him to escape.

The house of Hanover

George III wanted to be a farmer. George (ruled 1760 to 1820) lived during the Agricultural Revolution – a time when farmers were experimenting with new crops, techniques and machinery. George was most interested in these new developments. He liked to get away from London to countryside and talk to ordinary people.

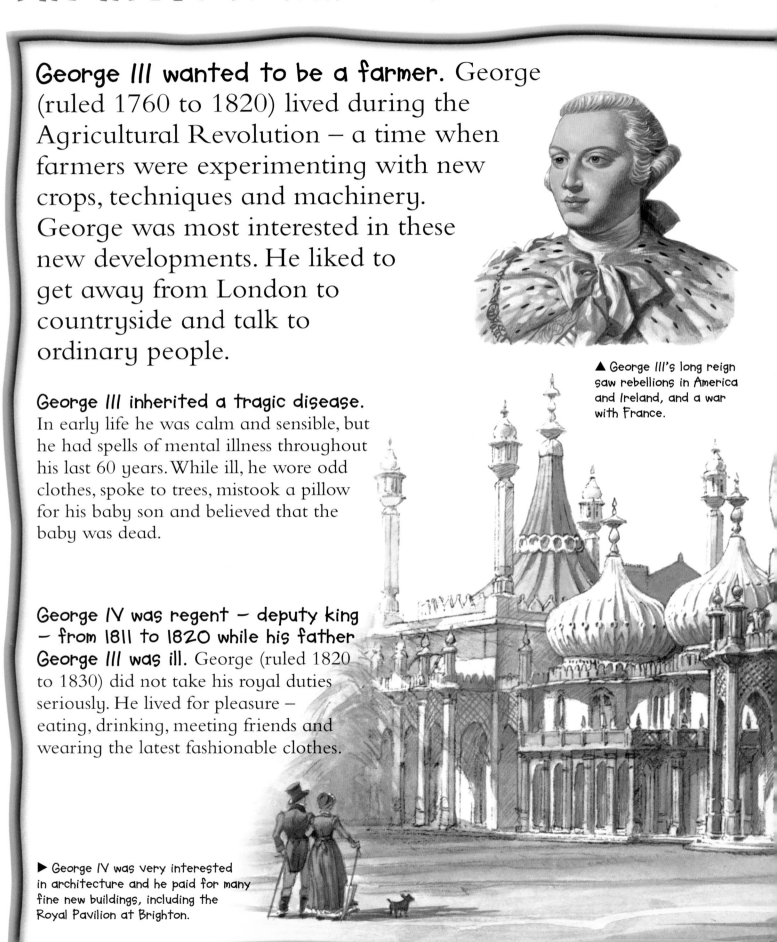

▲ George III's long reign saw rebellions in America and Ireland, and a war with France.

George III inherited a tragic disease. In early life he was calm and sensible, but he had spells of mental illness throughout his last 60 years. While ill, he wore odd clothes, spoke to trees, mistook a pillow for his baby son and believed that the baby was dead.

George IV was regent – deputy king – from 1811 to 1820 while his father George III was ill. George (ruled 1820 to 1830) did not take his royal duties seriously. He lived for pleasure – eating, drinking, meeting friends and wearing the latest fashionable clothes.

▶ George IV was very interested in architecture and he paid for many fine new buildings, including the Royal Pavilion at Brighton.

William IV served in the Royal Navy — then sailed into a political storm. When he became king in 1830, ordinary people were demanding the right to vote. Parliament wanted to allow this, but William disagreed. After a long quarrel with Parliament, William was forced to change his mind, earning the nickname 'Silly Billy'.

I DON'T BELIEVE IT!

Due to his size, George IV earned the nickname 'Prince of Whales' when he was Prince Regent.

Victoria and Albert

When Victoria became queen in 1837, many British people hated the monarchy. They were shocked and disgusted by lazy, greedy kings like her uncle, George IV. Victoria promised to do better. She worked very hard at learning how to be queen, and took a keen interest in politics and the law for the whole of her life.

Queen Victoria became 'the grandmother of Europe'. In 1840 Victoria married her cousin, Prince Albert. They were very happy together and had nine children. Because Britain was so powerful, many other European countries wanted to show friendship. So they arranged marriages between Victoria's children and their own royal families. By the time Victoria died her descendants ruled in Germany, Russia, Sweden, Denmark, Spain, Greece, Romania, Yugoslavia – and Britain!

▼ Prince Albert always gave Queen Victoria wise advice, and encouraged British science, industry and the arts.

Victoria's Britain was 'the workshop of the world'. British engineers and businessmen were world leaders in technology and manufacturing. They invented steam-powered machines to mass-produce goods in factories and steam-powered ships and locomotives to transport them round the world. In 1851 Prince Albert organized the Great Exhibition in London to display goods made in 'the workshop of the world'.

Victoria – 'the Widow of Windsor' or 'Mrs Brown'? Prince Albert died in 1861, aged 42. Victoria was grief-stricken. She dressed in black as a sign of mourning until she died in 1901. For many years, the only person who could comfort her was a Scottish servant, John Brown. Some people said that Victoria had fallen in love with her servant and they secretly called her 'Mrs Brown'.

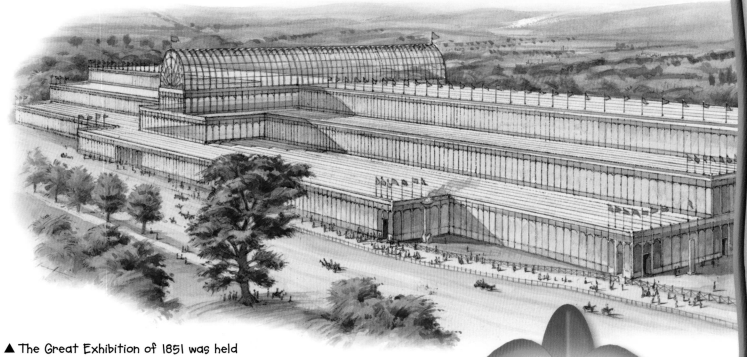

▲ The Great Exhibition of 1851 was held in a revolutionary new building – the Crystal Palace – made of iron and glass.

Queen Victoria ruled the largest empire in the world. It included most of the Indian subcontinent. Like many other British people, Victoria became fascinated by India's cultural heritage and rich civilization. She collected Indian jewels and art treasures and hired an Indian servant to teach her one of India's languages, Hindi.

ROYAL QUIZ

1. Who did Queen Victoria marry in 1840?

2. What did Prince Albert organize in 1851?

3. How many children did Queen Victoria have?

4. Who was John Brown?

Answers:
1. Prince Albert, her cousin
2. The Great Exhibition 3. Nine 4.
Queen Victoria's servant and friend

Edward VII waited sixty years before he became king. He spent a lot of his time, while waiting, having fun – he liked sailing, horse racing, gambling, fast cars and pretty women. But he also had a serious side. He spoke foreign languages very well and was a skilled politician and diplomat. After his mother, Queen Victoria, died, Edward reigned from 1901 to 1910.

◄ George V made the first royal Christmas broadcast to the people of Britain in 1932.

George V changed his name. Ever since Queen Victoria married Prince Albert, the British royal family had a German surname, Saxe-Coburg-Gotha. But in 1914 Britain and Germany went to war. So King George (ruled 1910 to 1936) changed his name to 'Windsor', the royal family's favourite home.

Edward VIII said 'something must be done'! In the 1920s and 1930s, Britain faced an economic crisis. Thousands of people lost their jobs. Edward felt sorry for them, and he visited poor communities. He caused a political row when he gave money to unemployed workers' families, and when he said that 'something must be done' by the government to help those out of work.

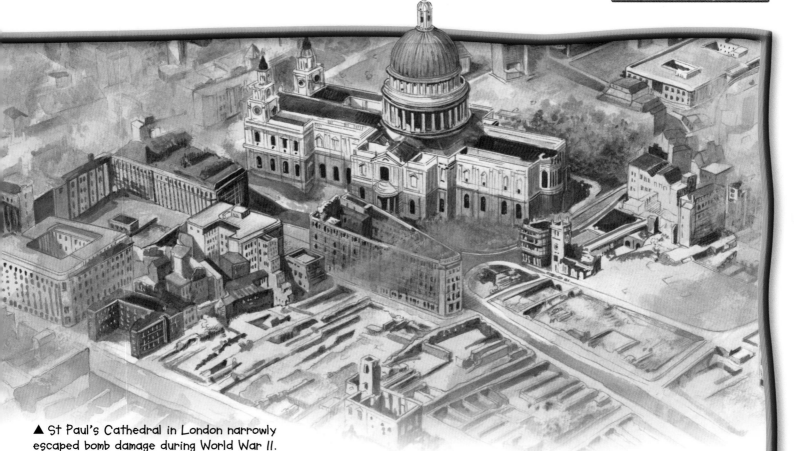

▲ St Paul's Cathedral in London narrowly escaped bomb damage during World War II.

Edward VIII gave up his throne for love. He became king in 1936 and immediately ran into trouble. He wanted to marry a divorced woman, Wallis Simpson, but the government, and the rest of the royal family, would not agree. So Edward abdicated (gave up the throne). He married Mrs Simpson, and spent the rest of his life living abroad.

George VI never expected to be king. But after Edward VIII abdicated he was next in line to the throne. George ruled from 1936 to 1952. Shy and with a stammer, George found royal duties difficult. People admired his devotion to duty and his settled family life.

London was a dangerous place during World War II. It was attacked by German warplanes. Many Londoners moved to the country but George VI and Queen Elizabeth, his wife, stayed in London to support the people, even after Buckingham Palace was bombed.

I DON'T BELIEVE IT!

George V had the best stamp collection in the world.

Queen Elizabeth II

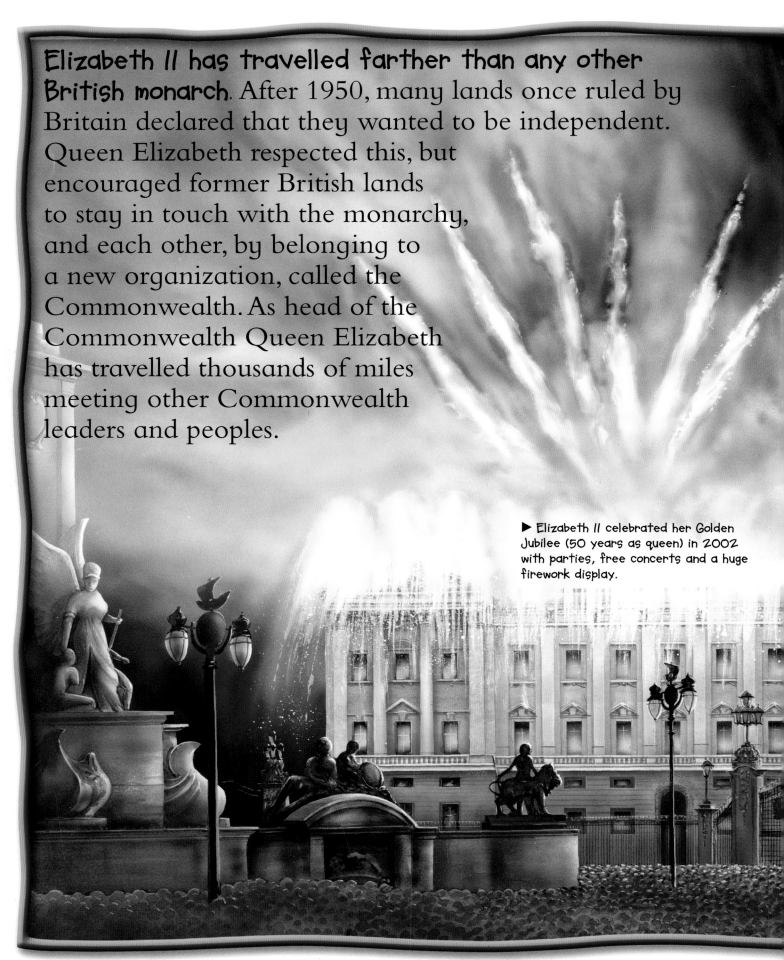

Elizabeth II has travelled farther than any other British monarch. After 1950, many lands once ruled by Britain declared that they wanted to be independent. Queen Elizabeth respected this, but encouraged former British lands to stay in touch with the monarchy, and each other, by belonging to a new organization, called the Commonwealth. As head of the Commonwealth Queen Elizabeth has travelled thousands of miles meeting other Commonwealth leaders and peoples.

▶ Elizabeth II celebrated her Golden Jubilee (50 years as queen) in 2002 with parties, free concerts and a huge firework display.

Queen Victoria came to the throne at a time of great change. The rural way of life that had existed for centuries was being swept away by the Industrial Revolution. Britain was being transformed into a bustling place that produced goods for everybody – the workshop of the world. During Victoria's 54-year reign, the rich became richer than they ever could have dreamed of, the poor faced almost unbearable poverty and Britain became the most powerful nation in the world. Victoria's coronation took place on 28 June 1838 at Westminster Abbey. Wrapped in a gold cloak and wearing a jewel-encrusted crown, Victoria was crowned queen.

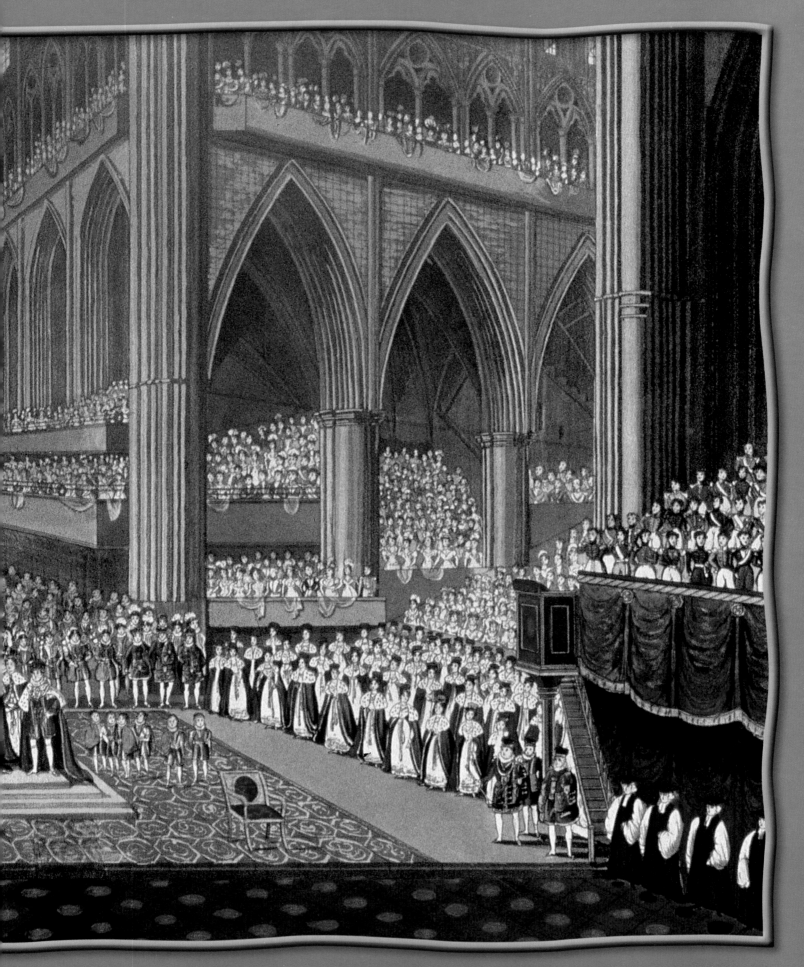

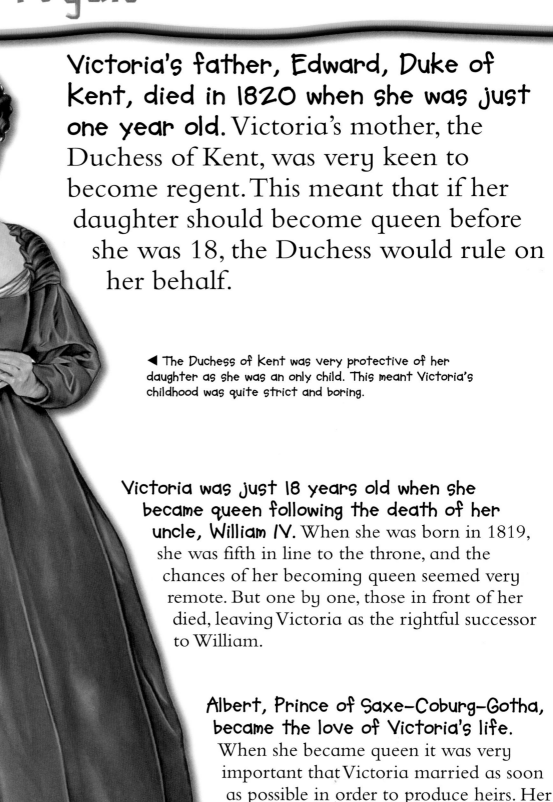

Victoria's father, Edward, Duke of Kent, died in 1820 when she was just one year old. Victoria's mother, the Duchess of Kent, was very keen to become regent. This meant that if her daughter should become queen before she was 18, the Duchess would rule on her behalf.

◄ The Duchess of Kent was very protective of her daughter as she was an only child. This meant Victoria's childhood was quite strict and boring.

Victoria was just 18 years old when she became queen following the death of her uncle, William IV. When she was born in 1819, she was fifth in line to the throne, and the chances of her becoming queen seemed very remote. But one by one, those in front of her died, leaving Victoria as the rightful successor to William.

Albert, Prince of Saxe-Coburg-Gotha, became the love of Victoria's life. When she became queen it was very important that Victoria married as soon as possible in order to produce heirs. Her advisors arranged for her to meet Albert, her handsome German cousin, and the couple fell deeply in love. They married in 1840 in a glittering ceremony at St James's Palace, London.

Victoria and Albert had a happy marriage and had nine children – five daughters and four sons. Their names were Vicky, Edward, Alice, Alfred, Helena, Louise, Arthur, Leopold and Beatrice. Some historians say that the queen was a stern mother, but others say she was warm and loving. Victoria was close to her daughter, Vicky, but had an uneasy relationship with her son, Edward.

I DON'T BELIEVE IT!

British law said that no man was allowed to propose to the queen, so Victoria had to ask for Albert's hand in marriage!

When Prince Albert died of typhoid at the age of 42, a Scottish gillie (servant) named John Brown became Victoria's most trusted friend. He befriended the queen during her period of mourning and even saved Victoria from an assassination attempt. Many people were suspicious of this close relationship, nicknaming the queen 'Mrs Brown'. When Victoria died, she was buried holding a photograph of her favourite servant.

▼ Like most families in the Victorian era, Victoria and Albert had many children. They valued family life and spent as much time as possible with their children. Sadly, three of Victoria's children died before she did – Alice, Leopold and Alfred.

The greatest Empire

The original founder of the British Empire was Queen Elizabeth I. She sent a series of explorers, including Sir Francis Drake, around the world to claim new lands for her kingdom. The Empire started life as a handful of colonies along the eastern coast of North America, but by the 1800s it had grown to include India, South Africa and Canada.

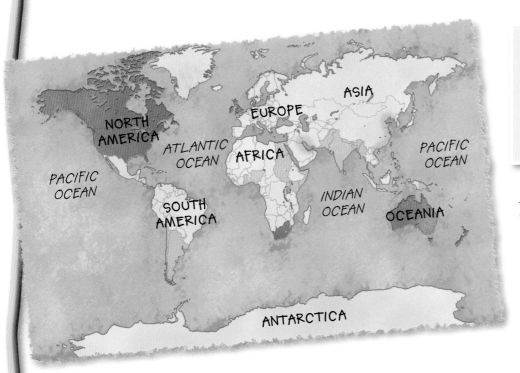

	English spoken as a first language
	English used in government
	English spoken among traders

◀ With the Empire at its height, English became the main spoken language of the British Isles, North America, the Caribbean and Oceania. English also became the language of government throughout much of Asia and Africa and was widely used by traders in non English-speaking areas.

During Victoria's reign, the British Empire expanded until it covered one-quarter of the world's surface. It also included all of the world's main trading routes, making Britain an extremely rich country. Victoria was proud of the British Empire, referring to it as the 'family of nations'.

India was the jewel of the British Empire. Elizabethan explorers arrived there in the 1500s, but for hundreds of years afterwards the country was ruled not by the queen, but by the British East India Company. In 1858 control passed to the British government after an uprising, and in 1877 Victoria became Empress of India in a lavish ceremony.

Many poorer people were desperate to escape poverty in Britain. Some made a fresh start by moving to a different part of the empire, emigrating as far as Australia and New Zealand. Others sought their fortune in the 'New World' of America, which called itself the land of opportunity and the land of the free.

Not every country in the empire was happy about being ruled by Britain. British soldiers were sent to all four corners of the empire to make sure countries obeyed Queen Victoria's laws. Towards the end of Victoria's rule, there were actually more British soldiers in larger countries such as India than there were back home.

▼ The Victorians in India practiced British customs such as drinking tea. Many Indians also adopted these customs.

QUIZ

1. Who was the original founder of the British Empire?

2. When did Queen Victoria become Empress of India?

3. Which British sport became popular in India?

4. Which British custom became widely practiced in India?

Answers:
1. Queen Elizabeth I 2. 1877
3. Cricket 4. Drinking tea

The British exported their way of life and customs to the countries in the empire. However, local people were allowed to follow their own customs as long as they didn't conflict with British law. New British-style buildings sprang up, and some local people spoke English as their first language. The colonies had their influence on Britain, too. Colonial fashion, such as the wearing of pyjamas, made their way back to Britain during Victoria's reign.

▼ Cricket became popular in India during Victoria's reign and is the number one sport there today.

Town and country

When Victoria came to the throne just 20 percent of the population lived in towns and cities. By the time she died, however, the number had reached 75 percent. London became the largest city in the world with a population of 6.5 million people. Overall, the number of people living in Britain had grown to 40 million.

Because only the rich could afford luxuries such as flushing toilets, Victorian streets stank with the smell of raw sewage. Poorer families made do with 'privvies' – closets made of earth or ash in huts in backyards. These were shared by several families.

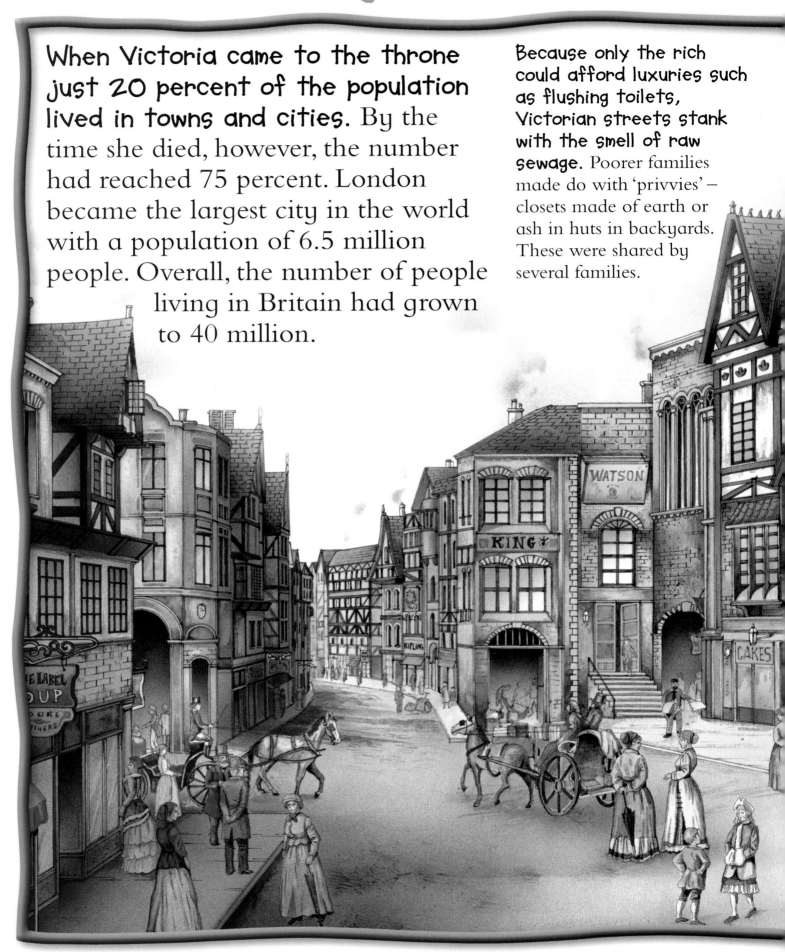

The Victorian poor often scratched a living by selling their wares on street corners. People also sold fruit and vegetables on market stalls, or traded bread, milk and pies from hand carts. There were also shoe-shiners who polished people's shoes and flower-sellers who sold posies to passers-by.

In the countryside, the craze for mechanization meant that machines were used to plough fields and carry out other duties. While this saved time, not everyone could afford these new advances in technology. For those farms that couldn't, many workers lost their jobs.

In 1846 the Corn Laws were abolished by Parliament. Originally brought in to protect farmers from cheap imported food, these laws raised food prices, causing great distress among the poor. When the Laws were removed, shoppers were delighted by the falling food bills, and this also created a bigger market for farmers to sell their produce.

◄ Many Victorian towns were overcrowded and polluted. Steets bustled with carriages and street-sellers. Lack of hygiene meant outbreaks of diseases such as cholera were common.

Rich and poor

The poor lived in dirty, back-to-back terrace houses with just four rooms at best. They had no running water and one house was often home to a husband and wife and up to ten children. Brothers and sisters had to share rooms and privacy was non-existent.

Homelessness was a growing problem in all the major cities. Those unable to work or too sick to enter the workhouse were thrown onto the streets. Many of the homeless were orphaned children. In 1867, Irishman Dr Thomas Barnado opened his first children's home in London to try and solve the problem.

▲ In Wales, Chartist protestors clashed with officials and many of the leaders of the movement were thrown into prison.

In the early years of Victoria's reign, Britain was in the grip of a depression. One group of people called the Chartists stirred up unrest by calling for the right to vote and demanding other reforms. Their fiery speeches caught the imagination of hungry audiences. Another movement, Marxism, proposed that everyone should be equal, all property should be owned by the State and that the monarchy should be abolished.

▼ Poor couples often had as many as ten children — they often went hungry.

The poor of Ireland suffered a disaster in the 1840s when a potato blight (disease) destroyed their crops. Millions of tonnes of potatoes were ruined and many people died from diseases such as scurvy as they had no other food source to provide them with vitamins. Thousands of people died of starvation, while others fled abroad. It took the government a long time to realize just how bad the problem was.

I DON'T BELIEVE IT!

Rich Victorian women had to suffer to look good — they wore whalebone corsets strengthened with steel that must have been agony to wear.

For the rich, Victorian Britain was a wonderful place to live. They went to the theatre, the opera, flocked to musicals and attended lavish charity events. This high life was enjoyed not just by lords and ladies but by a new group of people who had become wealthy through the Industrial Revolution.

The rich devoted a lot of time and money to looking good and living well. Ladies wore fabulous dresses and expensive jewellery (often imported from India), and carried fans from the Far East. Men wore spats to protect their shoes from mud and tucked expensive walking sticks under their arms whenever they went out.

◀ Ballroom dancing was a popular way for the rich to spend their evenings.

Get a job!

Factories and mills provided employment for the Victorian poor. Men and women would work all day on dangerous, smelly machinery making goods to sell around the world. In small clothing factories called sweatshops, poor workers were hustled into cramped, dingy rooms to work from dawn to dusk earning barely enough money to survive.

◄ By the 1850s, printing had been mechanized, which meant that books could be produced cheaply and quickly. Over 10,000 people in London were employed in the printing industry.

Mining was one of the deadliest jobs in Victorian Britain. Not only was there the constant threat of unstable shafts collapsing on workers, but pits sometimes filled up with explosive gases. To check for gas, miners often took canaries to work with them. If the birds stopped singing, it was seen as a sign that gas was present.

Going into service as a maid was the main career option for working-class girls. Work began at 6 a.m. and lasted until 10 p.m. Tasks ranged from stoking the fires and making the beds to serving meals and cleaning the house from top to bottom. Conditions for maids were harsh. They had no holidays, were forbidden from gossiping when on duty and often lived in freezing rooms without any form of heating, even in winter.

▶ Chimney sweep masters usually had child workers that they forced to climb up chimneys. Sometimes a fire was lit beneath the child to force them to climb higher.

In poor families, everybody worked, including children. Small boys and girls as young as five were sent up sooty chimneys to sweep them clean, crawled down dark mines or wriggled under factory machines to unpick tangled threads. Many of these jobs were dangerous and thousands of children died every year at work. In 1842, the Mines Act was passed, banning children from working in mines.

JOB JUMBLE

Here are seven jobs jumbled up. Can you work out what they are?

1. diam 2. radlpe
3 michyen weeps
4. reachet 5. renmi
6. codrot 7. ghannam

Answers:
1. Maid 2. Pedlar
3. Chimney sweep 4. Teacher
5. Miner 6. Doctor
7. Hangman

Some people who struggled to find full-time jobs became pedlars. These poor people trundled from town to town trying to make a living from selling their wares. Their numbers included rag-gatherers, bone-pickers, cloth-sellers and animal skin traders. Some ended up in prison as they were driven to crime by desperate poverty.

◀ This woman is selling fruit. She would have worked long hours every day for very little money.

Sent to the workhouse

The Poor Laws were made to encourage poor people to be less reliant on 'hand-outs'. This meant that to receive poor relief such as food or clothes, people had to live in the workhouse. The writer Charles Dickens (1812 to 1870) was so shocked by the conditions of workhouses that he wrote *Oliver Twist* to highlight the problem. He campaigned throughout his lifetime to turn public opinion against these terrible places.

▲ Charles Dickens wrote mainly about the problems of Victorian Britain, and in particular the desperate conditions of the poor.

▼ A scene from the 1968 musical *Oliver!*, based on Charles Dickens' novel *Oliver Twist*. The book tells the tale of a young orphan boy sent to a London workhouse.

Victorian authorities viewed poverty as a result of laziness, drunkenness and vice, and poor people were afraid of ending up in the workhouse. Inmates were separated from their families and were fed so little that many were literally starving. In one workhouse in Andover, Hampshire, people were seen scavenging for meat on the bones they were being forced to grind to make fertilizer.

▼ Food in the workhouse consisted mainly of a watery soup called gruel, and bread and cheese.

PUNISHMENT!

The scold's bridle was a particularly nasty punishment for badly behaved workhouse inmates. What did it stop the wearer doing?
a) Moving
b) Speaking
c) Eating
d) Crying

Answer:
b) it stopped the wearer from talking

Children without fathers were sent to the workhouse with their mothers if the family was too poor to support them. The Victorian public were shocked by such cruelty, however, and the law was changed to allow single mothers to make fathers pay towards the upkeep of their children.

The treatment in workhouses was harsh, and children were often beaten for misbehaving. At the Marylebone Workhouse in London, a scandal was caused by the number of children who ended up in hospital or even dead as a result of their terrible mistreatment.

Get me a doctor

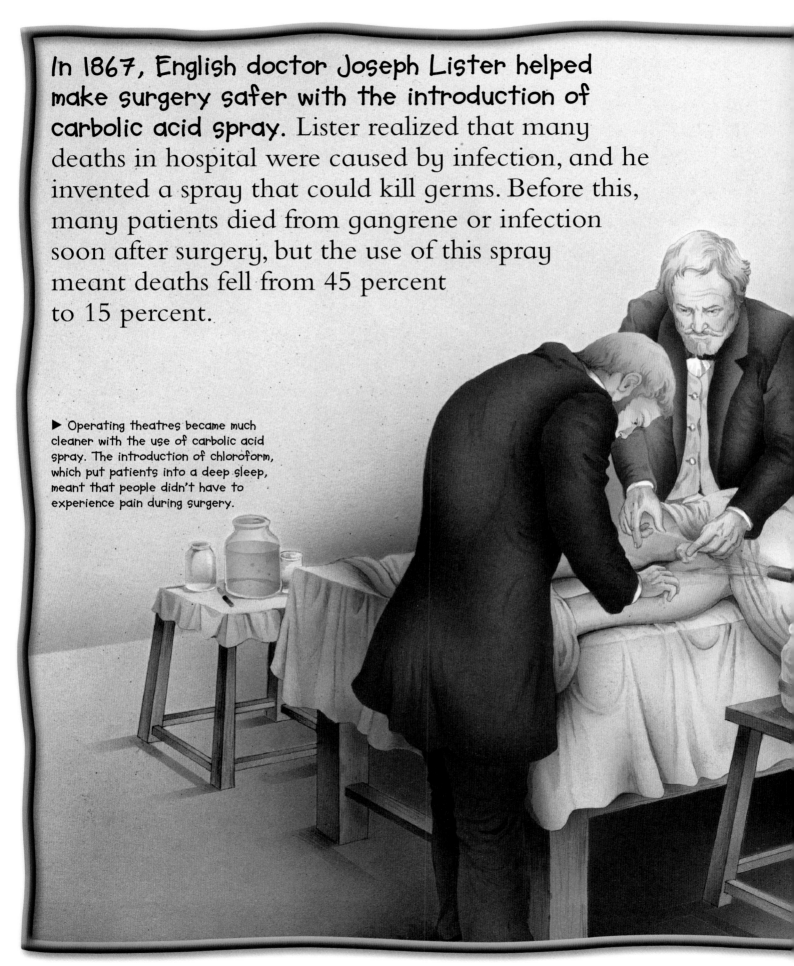

In 1867, English doctor Joseph Lister helped make surgery safer with the introduction of carbolic acid spray. Lister realized that many deaths in hospital were caused by infection, and he invented a spray that could kill germs. Before this, many patients died from gangrene or infection soon after surgery, but the use of this spray meant deaths fell from 45 percent to 15 percent.

▶ Operating theatres became much cleaner with the use of carbolic acid spray. The introduction of chloroform, which put patients into a deep sleep, meant that people didn't have to experience pain during surgery.

Around 1850, the Scottish doctor Alexander Wood (1817 to 1884), invented the hypodermic syringe. The hollow, pointed needle (which could puncture the skin painlessly) was used to inject powerful painkilling drugs such as morphine and opium.

Victorian doctors made surgery less painful. For hundreds of years, patients had died on the operating table from shock. In 1847 an English doctor, John Snow, started using a chemical called chloroform that made people sleep during surgery. Queen Victoria's doctor persuaded the queen to use the drug during the birth of Prince Leopold in 1853.

Doctors William Budd and John Snow prevented many Victorians dying from drinking dirty water. The two men realized that diseases such as cholera were carried in water, and they encouraged authorities to shut down infected pumps. The doctors' actions helped to dramatically reduce the number of deaths from water-borne diseases.

I DON'T BELIEVE IT!

The Victorian age also saw the first dentist's drill and the first porcelain false teeth!

Bright ideas

During the reign of Queen Victoria, Britain was full of people with clever ideas. Prince Albert was so impressed with the inventiveness of the Victorians that he held the Great Exhibition to show off their work. In 1851, over 14,000 men and women gathered in the newly built iron and glass Crystal Palace to show off their gadgets to millions of dazzled visitors.

William Cook and Charles Wheatstone invented the Victorian Internet – the electric telegraph. In 1837 the two Englishmen started to send messages down metal lines using electricity. In 1866, telegraph lines were laid under the Atlantic Ocean all the way to Canada using the first submarines.

▼ The Crystal Palace was a vast building, three times the length of St Paul's Cathedral and covered an area of 26 acres.

Joseph Swan brightened up Victorian houses in 1879 with the first working electric light bulb. By running electricity through a piece of wire called a filament inside a glass bulb, he was able to produce light. In 1883, Swan joined forces with the American Thomas Edison to create the Edison and Swan United Electric Lighting Company.

▼ Joseph Swan invented the lightbulb in 1860. The first filaments were made of paper coated in carbon.

▼ Victorians often looked stern and solemn in photographs because it took so long to expose the pictures — imagine having to pose a smile for up to one minute!

Vain Victorians were thrilled with the arrival of the first easy-to-use camera. In July 1857 Queen Victoria and her family posed for photographs using one of John Herschel and William Henry Fox Talbot's devices.

▶ As well as coming up with the idea of the telephone, Alexander Graham Bell also went on to invent the world's first method of recording sound, the gramophone.

Brilliant Scot Alexander Graham Bell came up with an invention that changed the world — the telephone. By transmitting speech electronically down wires, the telephone allowed people to talk to each other no matter where they were in the world. The first telephone call took place in 1876, when Bell rang his assistant and spoke the words, "Come here Watson, I want you." Bell's invention was so popular that by 1887 there were over 26,000 telephones in Britain.

Getting around

Victorian steam trains hurtled along their tracks. By 1900, 35,000 kilometres of track had been laid in Britain, while in 1863 the world's first underground station had opened in London as railways continued to develop at breakneck speed. One of the most famous routes ran from the West Country to London, and was designed by the engineer Isambard Kingdom Brunel (1806 to 1859). Passengers were so impressed that the Great Western Railway earned the nickname of 'God's Wonderful Railway'.

▲ Brunel was a great engineer who built ocean liners and bridges as well as railways.

In the same year that Victoria was crowned queen, the biggest ship in the world, the *Great Western*, set sail. It was a 1200-tonne monster – the biggest ship in the world. *The Great Western* sailed for the first time on 19 July 1837, and reached the USA in April 1838.

Inventors were also trying to take to the air during Victoria's reign. In 1853 Sir George Cayley persuaded a servant to fly a glider across a valley in Yorkshire. Barely rising above head height, the machine flew 200 metres before crashing into nearby trees.

I DON'T BELIEVE IT!
Some people thought that travelling on the fastest Victorian trains would lead to instant death by suffocation!

Better roads meant that more and more cars were also taking to the roads. The first practical motor vehicles appeared around 1895, and tarmac on roads meant that driving became a far more comfortable experience!

◀ The Great Western railway gave people freedom. For the first time it was possible to travel from Bristol to London and back in one day.

Telling tales

The most famous storyteller in Victorian Britain was Charles Dickens. Fascinated by the poor areas of London, Dickens would pound the streets at night, making notes of what he saw. As well as Oliver Twist, Dickens wrote other classics such as *The Pickwick Papers, A Christmas Carol, David Copperfield* and *Great Expectations*.

▲ Dickens' *A Christmas Carol* tells the story of Scrooge, a miserly old man who is visited by a succession of ghosts on Christmas Eve.

Three sisters raised in a bleak house on the windswept Yorkshire moors went on to become some of the greatest writers in Victorian Britain. Charlotte, Emily and Anne Brontë wrote classics such as *Wuthering Heights, Jane Eyre* and *The Tenant of Wildfell Hall.* The three sisters all died young within seven years of each other.

▶ Stevenson's *The Strange Case of Dr Jekyll and Mr Hyde* explores how things are not always quite what they seem on the surface. The novel was also adapted into various screen versions, one of which is advertised by this poster.

▶ In 1846, the Brontë sisters had a joint volume of poems published under the pen names of Currer, Ellis and Acton Bell. At the time they had to use men's names to be taken seriously as authors.

Robert Louis Stevenson (1772 to 1850) could write at an astonishing speed. The Scottish novelist wrote *The Strange Case of Dr Jekyll and Mr Hyde* – a story of a doctor who turns into Mr Hyde, a nasty character, after drinking a potion. Stevenson also wrote *Treasure Island* and *Kidnapped*, all about pirate adventures.

Irishman Oscar Wilde was born in Dublin in 1854. In 1878 he moved to London to seek success as a writer and playwright. His most famous play was *The Importance of Being Earnest*, about the excesses of Victorian society. Wilde also wrote a novel, *The Picture of Dorian Gray*, and a collection of fairy tales.

Lewis Carroll (1832 to 1898) was the pen name of the Reverend Charles Lutwidge Dodgson. Although he never married, Carroll loved children, and wrote books including *Alice in Wonderland* and *Through the Looking Glass* for the daughters of friends. Carroll also wrote nonsense verse, including the poem 'Jabberwocky'.

In 1887, Irishman Bram Stoker (1847 to 1912) created one of the most terrifying horror stories ever written. *Dracula* is a tale about a vampire, based on east European legends, who lured victims to his castle in Transylvania to drink their blood so as to stay forever young. He had the power to turn himself into a bat, and could only be killed by driving a stake through his heart.

◀ *Dracula* has been made into dozens of films. This 1968 version starred Christopher Lee as Count Dracula.

▼ The Mad Hatter's tea party, where Alice takes tea with a collection of bizarre characters, is one of the most famous parts of Carroll's *Alice in Wonderland*.

ANAGRAM AGONY

Rearrange the sentences below to find the names of four famous books.

1. Wives tor lit
2. Any jeeer
3. Ada curl
4. In an odd wine cellar

Answers:
1. *Oliver Twist* 2. *Jane Eyre* 3. *Dracula* 4. *Alice in Wonderland*

Build it!

Gothic was all the rage while Victoria was in power. Many architects copied this 13th-century style of architecture, creating buildings with pointed arches and high spires. The most famous examples are the new Houses of Parliament, the University of Glasgow and St Pancras Station in London.

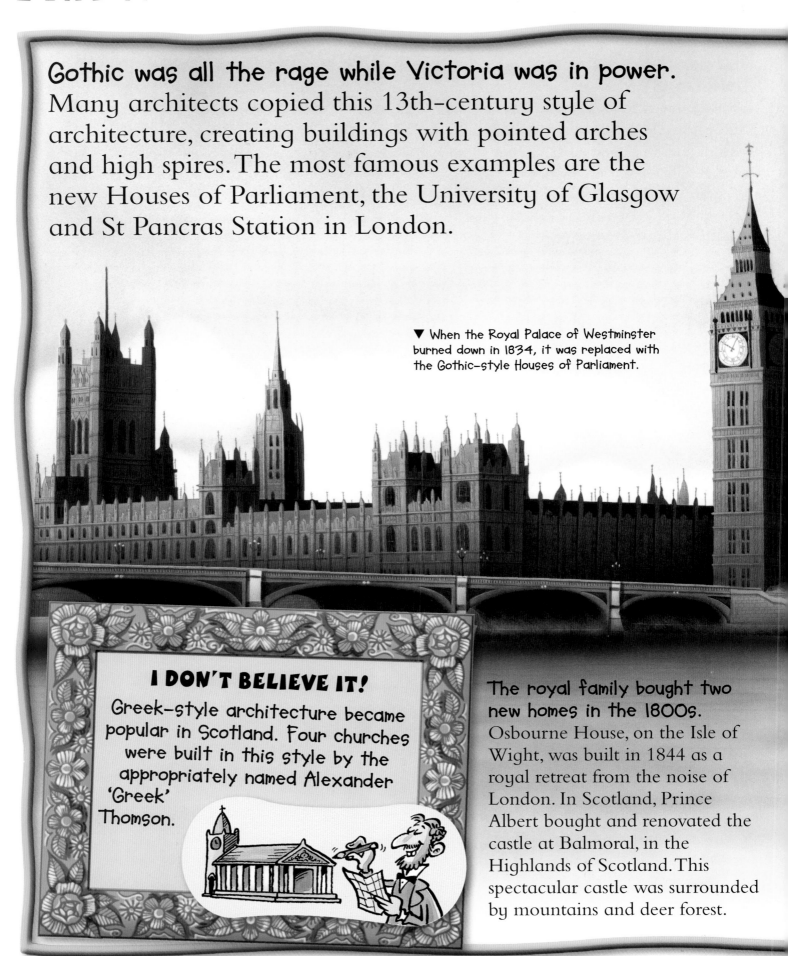

▼ When the Royal Palace of Westminster burned down in 1834, it was replaced with the Gothic-style Houses of Parliament.

I DON'T BELIEVE IT!

Greek-style architecture became popular in Scotland. Four churches were built in this style by the appropriately named Alexander 'Greek' Thomson.

The royal family bought two new homes in the 1800s. Osbourne House, on the Isle of Wight, was built in 1844 as a royal retreat from the noise of London. In Scotland, Prince Albert bought and renovated the castle at Balmoral, in the Highlands of Scotland. This spectacular castle was surrounded by mountains and deer forest.

The Victorians loved to build with iron and glass. Dramatic arched iron bridges strode across Britain's rivers, while at the Royal Botanic Gardens in Kew, an iron and glass frame protected the palm house from the harsh weather outside. Probably the most famous iron and glass building was the Crystal Palace, built to house the Great Exhibition in 1851. Sadly it burnt to the ground just a few years later.

In Scotland, architect Charles Rennie Mackintosh was building great buildings out of stone blocks. He designed the interior of the Willow Tea Rooms in Glasgow and filled it with mirrors and stencilled figures, created by his wife Margaret Macdonald. Mackintosh's best-known work was the Glasgow School of Art building, an imposing stone building that was begun in 1897.

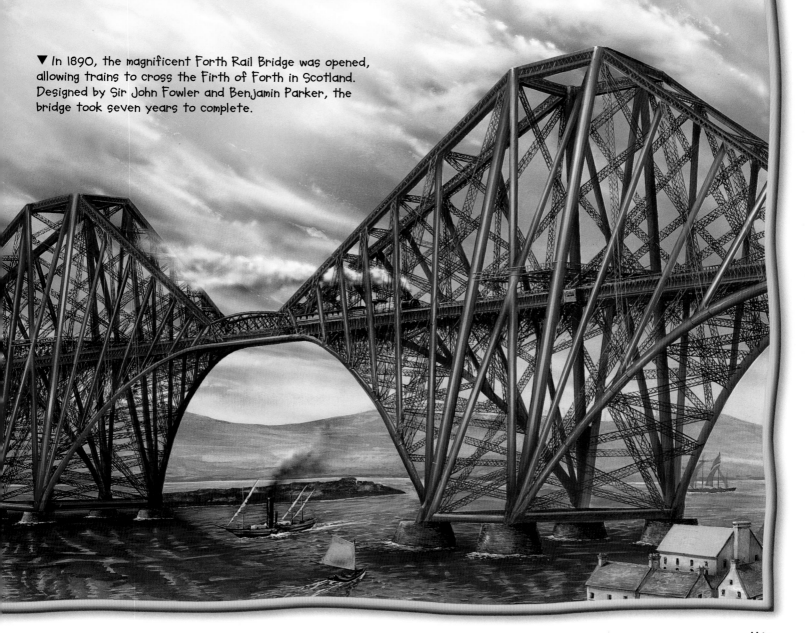

▼ In 1890, the magnificent Forth Rail Bridge was opened, allowing trains to cross the Firth of Forth in Scotland. Designed by Sir John Fowler and Benjamin Parker, the bridge took seven years to complete.

What's for dinner?

Cooks in the 1800s had a problem keeping food fresh. Meat or fish would go off after a few days, or even sooner in hot weather. To solve this problem, Victorian inventors built the first refrigerator in 1900. Food was chilled by cold air, circulated by a pump from ice blocks stored in a special compartment. Scientists also found a way to tin food, meaning that groceries such as fruit and vegetables could be kept fresh for months.

Children throughout Victorian Britain were delighted by the arrival of ice-cream. A famous cook called Agnes Marshall set up her own cookery school specializing in the delicious dessert. She claims to have made the first ice-cream cornet in 1888 and published a book called *Fancy Ices* in 1894.

▼ Victorian cooks worked extremely hard. All food was prepared by hand — from bread to soup and puddings.

Exotic foods brought back from the farthest corners of the Empire ended up on the dining tables of the wealthy. Fruits such as pineapples and kiwi became popular with the rich, while spices such as turmeric found their way into Victorian cooking pots. Tea, for a long time a luxury, became affordable for everybody.

Pineapple

Tea

Kiwi fruit

Turmeric

▶ Pineapples were brought to Britain from the Caribbean, kiwi fruit from New Zealand and turmeric and tea from India.

Fresh milk was delivered straight from the farm to the doors of Victorian houses. On set days, householders would carry out jugs to the passing milkman, who filled them from large churns. The ready availability of milk added Vitamin D to the diets of many malnourished children, helping to prevent diseases such as rickets.

Mrs Beeton became the world's first celebrity chef. The eldest girl among 17 children, she spent most of her childhood bringing up her younger brothers and sisters. She went on to find work as a magazine editor, and had the idea of collecting recipes sent in by readers to make into a book. In 1861, Mrs Beeton published *Mrs Beeton's Book of Household Management*, packed with recipes and tips.

▶ Victorian milkmen usually carried milk in large open pails hung from a wooden yoke across their shoulders.

MAKE ICE CREAM!
You will need:
large plastic bag   ice   6 tbsp salt   1 tbsp sugar   ½ pint milk vanilla essence   bowl small plastic bag

1. Half fill the larger bag with ice, add the salt and seal it.

2. Mix the sugar with the milk and vanilla in a bowl, pour into the small bag and seal it.

3. Open the large bag, put the small bag inside and seal the large bag again.

4. Shake the bag for a few minutes. Your mixture will turn to ice cream!

Let us pray

Around 60 percent of Victorians regularly went to church on Sundays. New churches were built and old ones restored to cope with a religious revival. A bill to force people to attend church on Sundays was put forward in 1837, and Victorian society expected people to be hardworking and respectable.

▲ The Salvation Army helped the poor and needy. These London school children are enjoying breakfast supplied by army members in 1900.

English religious leader William Booth founded the Christian Mission in East London in 1865, which was renamed the Salvation Army in 1878. This army did not fight with bullets and swords but with the word of God. Booth organized members like an army to fight against sin and evil. The Salvation Army's aim was to show the love of God through Christianity and concern for the poorer classes.

◀ At the age of 13 William Booth was sent to work as an apprentice in a pawnbroker's shop. This experience helped him to understand the suffering endured by the Victorian poor.

Many Victorians thought the Church of England was neglecting the poor. The new Evangelical Church had a more caring attitude towards the less well-off and placed emphasis on helping the needy. It had also been responsible for pressing the government to abolish slavery throughout the Empire.

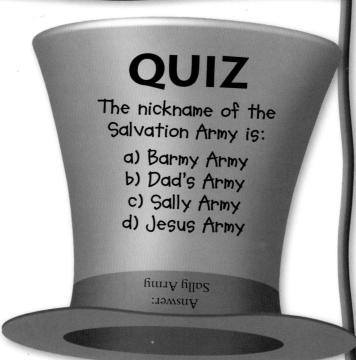

▲ The remote Galapagos Islands are situated off the West coast of Ecuador. This map charts the route that Darwin took in his ship *The Beagle*.

In 1859, Charles Darwin published *Origin of Species*, throwing religious leaders into a fury. The book challenged the accepted idea that God created the world. In 1871, Darwin published *The Descent of Man*, which said that man evolved gradually from apes thousands of years ago. Darwin developed his ideas during a trip to the Galapagos Islands in South America, where he noticed that a single species of bird had evolved into many different kinds to adapt to different habitats.

Religious beliefs were also challenged by the discovery of dinosaur fossils. Finding fossils of creatures that lived millions of years before man was a shock, especially when the Bible said the world was created just a few thousand years ago. People found their religious faith being tested.

▼ The skull of the dinosaur *Heterodontosaurus*. Finding ancient fossil remains such as this made people question what was written in the Bible.

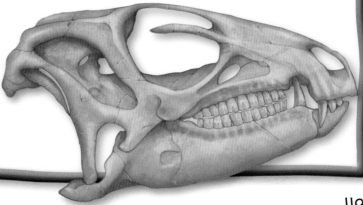

The long arm of the law

By 1856 most towns had their own police force. The first police officers wore top hats and tailcoats, and wielded wooden truncheons. They were known as 'peelers' or 'bobbies' after Sir Robert Peel, who set up London's Metropolitan police force in 1829.

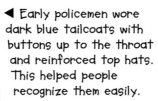
◀ Early policemen wore dark blue tailcoats with buttons up to the throat and reinforced top hats. This helped people recognize them easily.

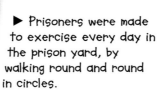
▶ Prisoners were made to exercise every day in the prison yard, by walking round and round in circles.

The Victorians built lots of new prisons. Old gaols and rusting prison hulks (ships) could not cope with the crime rate, so between 1842 and 1877, 90 new lock-ups were built. Life inside was hard work and prisoners were not allowed to talk to each other. The aim was to make prisoners think about what they had done and face up to their responsibilities.

You could be locked up for not paying your debts in Victorian Britain. Houses of Correction such as Fleet, Clink and Marshalsea prisons in London held beggars, the homeless and those who owed money. They stayed behind bars until their debts were settled.

Less people were sentenced to death in Victorian Britain than in the past. But it still remained the ultimate punishment. To make death more 'humane', trap doors were installed on the gallows, breaking the victims' necks more quickly when they dropped to their deaths.

▶ The sentence for a murderer was death by hanging.

Pickpockets were a plague in large Victorian towns. Professional thieves used their quick fingers to lift items such as jewellery from wealthy victims, often followimg men and women out of pubs, as drunken people made easier victims.

▼ Gangs of child pickpockets run by violent criminals were found in all the large cities in Britain.

Science was helping to catch criminals for the first time. In 1884 Sir Francis Dalton proposed the use of fingerprints to identify criminals, and soon after, detectives became able to spot the tiniest specks of blood on criminals' clothing. There were also methods for detecting the use of poisons. Less successful ways to catch villains included physiology and the studying of prisoners' bodies to try to prove that they 'looked' different from ordinary people.

I DON'T BELIEVE IT!

People were so gripped by Sir Arthur Conan Doyle's stories about the fictional detective Sherlock Holmes that some were convinced he was a real policeman!

The most famous villain in Victorian Britain was never caught by the police. Jack the Ripper killed at least five women in East London in 1888. The killer also sent postcards to the police to taunt them, but he was never identified.

That'll teach them

In 1880, a new law stating that all children between the ages of five and ten must go to school, came into force. Because education was not free, however, few poor families could afford to send their children to school. In 1891, the law was changed again and schooling up to the age of 11 became free for all.

In 1818, a Portsmouth shoemaker called John Pounds started a free school for poor children. The idea was copied by others, and by 1852 there were over 200 of these 'ragged schools' in Britain. Conditions were often very basic. When Charles Dickens visited a ragged school in the 1840s he was said to be appalled by the state of the buildings and how dirty the children were.

▼ Victorian lessons concentrated on the 'three Rs' — Reading, wRiting and aRithmetic. Children learned by repeating lines until they were word perfect.

Many working-class children had to work all week, and had little chance to learn. Sunday (or Charity) schools were set up to try to give these children a basic education. Children were taught how to read and write, and attended Bible study classes.

▶ School children sat in rows at wooden desks, facing the blackboard. They wrote onto a slate using slate pencils.

Naughty Victorian children faced punishments at school. Stern schoolmasters punished disobedient or disruptive children with the strap and the cane for 'crimes' such as leaving the playground without permission. Some teachers hit pupils so hard their canes snapped. To stop this happening, they stored their canes in jars of water to make them more supple!

I DON'T BELIEVE IT!

The most famous pickpocket is a character from *Oliver*. The Artful Dodger is a member of Fagin's gang, which gets Oliver into trouble.

▼ If children were particularly poor at a lesson such as maths, they would be made to sit in the corner wearing this dunce's hat! Sums were done using an abacus, a wooden frame with beads for counting.

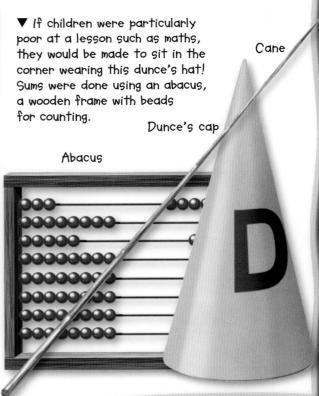

Cane

Dunce's cap

Abacus

End of an era

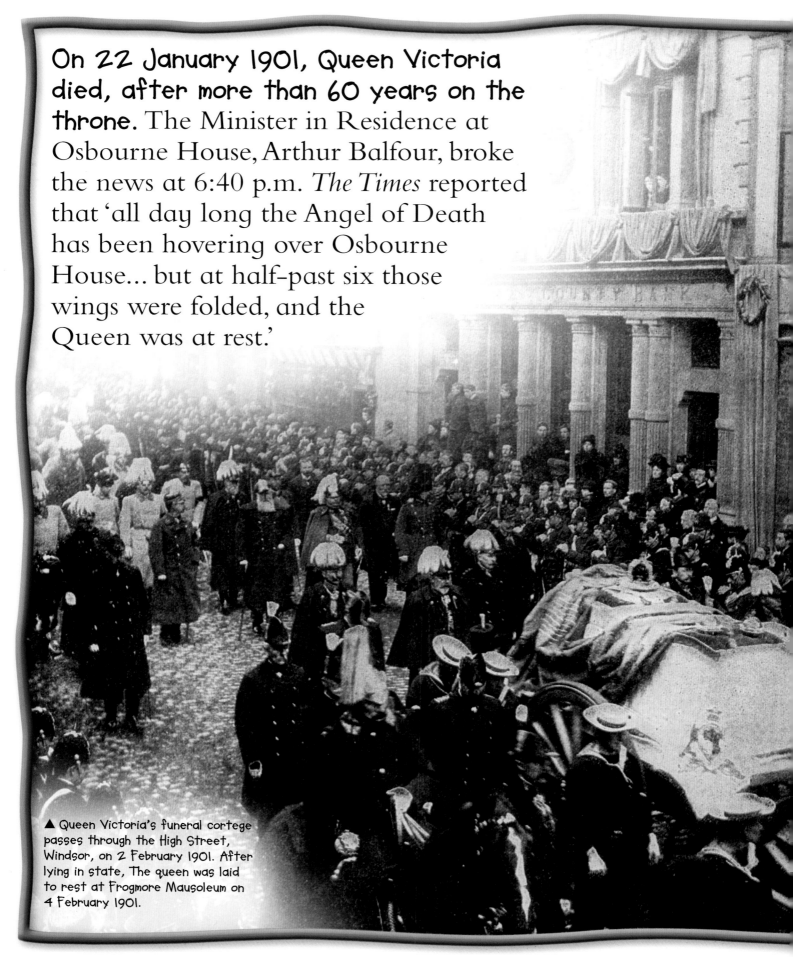

On 22 January 1901, Queen Victoria died, after more than 60 years on the throne. The Minister in Residence at Osbourne House, Arthur Balfour, broke the news at 6:40 p.m. *The Times* reported that 'all day long the Angel of Death has been hovering over Osbourne House... but at half-past six those wings were folded, and the Queen was at rest.'

▲ Queen Victoria's funeral cortege passes through the High Street, Windsor, on 2 February 1901. After lying in state, The queen was laid to rest at Frogmore Mausoleum on 4 February 1901.

After Victoria's death the throne passed to her son, Edward VII. Victoria had never trusted Edward, and had prevented him from interfering in important issues during her lifetime. When he became king, however, Edward devoted himself to his country, and became well-liked by the British public and across Europe.

◄ Kaiser Wilhelm II of Germany. Some people blamed the Kaiser for the start of World War I.

▲ Edward VII proved to be a good foreign ambassador for Britain as he was related to many of the European royal houses.

When he became king, Edward VII faced an immediate challenge from Germany. Led by Kaiser Wilhelm II, Victoria's grandson, the country began building its fleet of ships until it rivalled the Royal Navy in size. Four years after Edward died, the two countries were at war with each other.

King Edward VII tried to make life better for ordinary people. In 1902 he supported a new law making secondary education cheaper, and helped establish old age pensions in 1908. Despite this, the divide between rich and poor continued to grow, and it was not until the World War 1 in 1914 that people began to question their positions in society.

I DON'T BELIEVE IT!

When Victoria's death was announced, people wore black, and black and purple banners were hung from shop windows. Iron fences were given a fresh coat of black paint to mark the occasion.

INDEX

ACKNOWLEDGEMENTS

All artworks are from the Miles Kelly Artwork Bank

The publishers would like to thank the following sources for the use of their photographs:

t = top, b = bottom, l = left, r = right, c = centre

Corbis
Page 92 Hulton Deutsch Collection/CORBIS; 109 Hulton Deutsch Collection/CORBIS

Fotoware
Page 122 Fotoware a.s 1997–2003

Pictorial Press
Page 104 Columbia; 108; 112 Paramount; 113 Rank; 118(bl); 124; 125

The Salvation Army International Heritage Centre
Page 118(tr)

Topfoto
Cover (b/g) Topfoto, (main) Topham Picturepoint

All other photographs are from: Corel, digitalSTOCK, digitalvision, ImageState, iStockphoto.com, John Foxx, PhotoAlto, PhotoDisc, PhotoEssentials, PhotoPro, Stockbyte

Every effort has been made to acknowledge the source and copyright holder of each picture. Miles Kelly Publishing apologises for any unintentional errors or omissions.